ATHEISM AND THEISM

ATHEISM AND THEISM

ERROL E. HARRIS

HUMANITIES PRESS

NEW JERSEY

Originally published in 1977 as Volume XXVI of
Tulane Studies in Philosophy

This paperback edition first published 1993 by Humanities Press
International, Inc.,
Atlantic Highlands, New Jersey 07716

Library of Congress Cataloging-in-Publication Data
Harris, Errol E.
Atheism and theism / Errol E. Harris
p. cm.
"Originally published in 1977 as volume XXVI of Tulane studies in
philosophy" — T.p. verso.
ISBN 0–391–03799–4
1. Atheism. 2. Theism. I. Title.
BL2747.3.H37 1993
211′.3—dc20 92–32787
CIP

A catalog record for this book is available from the British Library

Printed in the United States of America

CONTENTS

PREFACE

This book is in some sense a sequel and supplement to *Revelation through Reason,*[1] which was written twenty years earlier. For long I have wished to write a book on the philosophy of religion, but have always deferred the task until I should have time to read sufficiently widely in theology to deal adequately with the subject. Other pursuits have persistently prevented my devoting time to this research and much of the intended discussion, for instance of Kierkegaard, Karl Barth and Emil Brunner, has now been forestalled by Brand Blanshard's exhaustive study in *Reason and Belief*. Five years ago, however, I was asked to review Sir Malcolm Knox' Gifford Lectures, *A Layman's Quest*[2] and despite my great admiration for the book, I was impressed by an omission which seemed to me of great importance. Sir Malcolm addressed himself to the historical development of biblical criticism and sought to answer the question: 'What is it reasonable to believe?' But he dealt only with the doctrines of believers and made no attempt to answer those, of whom today there are many, who consider it unreasonable to believe in God at all or to accept any religious doctrine. Those influenced by Hume and Russell, and even more those who give weight and credence to the writings of Nietzsche, Marx, Freud and Sartre, would not even begin to consider arguments such as Sir Malcolm's nor show any interest in discussions of biblical criticism. Accordingly, when I was invited to deliver the Matchette Lectures at Tulane University I chose the subject, Atheism and Theism, and the contents of the first three chapters of this book cover the subject matter of those lectures.

But they ended inconclusively, though the conclusion suggested was easily apparent, and I thought it necessary to develop it explicitly. In doing so, I had to face the implicit critique of my own views in Blanshard's *Reason and Belief*, which I have

[1] Yale University Press, New Haven, and Allen and Unwin, London, 1958.
[2] Allen and Unwin, London, 1969. The Review appeared under the title 'Reasonable Belief' in *Religious Studies*, Vol. 8, 1972.

vii

tried to meet in the final chapters. I took the opportunity also
of expanding and supplementing the arguments first presented
in *Revelation through Reason,* which on the subject of evil,
had already been carried a stage further in Chapter VII, §7,
of *Salvation from Despair.*[1] This topic was taken up afresh in
my Aquinas Lectures, at Marquette University.[2] The final
chapter continues and expands the argument put forward in
the fifth chapter of *Revelation through Reason,* again taking
into consideration and endeavouring to refute fresh objections
raised, not directly to my own writings, but to the position and
theses that I want to maintain.

The outcome is not so complete and exhaustive a treatment
as I could have wished of the reconciliation of faith and reason,
but I hope it is sufficient to reveal the bankruptcy of the
atheistic position and to demonstrate the clear possibility of
giving a rational interpretation of the main Christian doctrine.
Rational interpretation is not, of course, to be confused with
what is commonly understood by 'Rationalism'. That is all too
often a short-sighted and obtuse reliance on a superficial consistency, which, when pressed, breaks down in disastrous self-
contradiction, and which is often coupled with a form of 'hard-
headedness' that takes all symbolism as literal description and
reads metaphor as arrant nonsense. Such 'rationalism' I have
attempted, both here and elsewhere, to expose for what it is,
a provisional and immature phase in the development of reason,
to be approved as an antidote to superstition, sentimentality
and obscurantism, but to be recognized as a mere half-way
stage on the road to a deeper and more secure rational insight.

In these pages I have used the word 'theism' in a sense which
does not seem to be that commonly adopted. Apart from the
very general sense of belief in God, I do not understand theism
as the traditional conception of a God separate from a world
which he has created by a voluntary act. That I have called
(elsewhere) Deism, and in *Revelation through Reason* I made
the distinction explicit.[3] By theism I understand the conception
of and belief in an infinite and transcendent God, supernatural

[1] Nijhoff, The Hague, 1973.
[2] Marquette Univ. Press, Milwaukee, 1977.
[3] *Op. cit.,* (London 1958), pp. 34ff.

only in the sense that he transcends all finites which comprise the natural world, including the endlessly finite, which is commonly called infinite. God must be immanent and all inclusive as well as transcendent, for otherwise his infinitude cannot be maintained. A God separate from the world, even a world he has himself created, is not infinite, first because without the creation he would lack something, and if he lacked nothing would have no pretext to create; secondly because the world which he excludes would be (so far as excluded) a limitation upon his being and a negation of it. The infinite then would have to include both God and world and would be identical with neither.

The God of traditional religion has been variously conceived in different places and at different times, often inadequately; but every developed religion recognizes that nothing is worthy of man's worship short of an infinite being. The worship of anything less is idolatry. The reason for this is that man himself, being conscious of himself and the world, and capable of intelligence, finds no limit in principle to his own aspirations, and consequently nothing to which he can appropriately submit and genuinely revere except what is absolutely infinite.

Genuine belief in God, therefore, however its object may be misconceived, through ignorance, misapprehension, or confused imagining, to which all men are subject in some degree, is ultimately and in principle theism in my understanding of that word; and all inadequate concepts of God, when their shortcomings are remedied and contradictions removed, lead to what Anselm expressed in his formula: 'that than which a greater cannot be conceived'.

Atheism is the denial of the existence of any god whatsoever. The non-existence of God may be only an initial presumption, in which case it is equivalent to agnosticism and Cartesian doubt; but atheism proper is a claim to knowledge. Antony Flew wishes to distinguish the first case from agnosticism on the ground that the agnostic is one who has considered the question whether God exists, and thus claims to have a legitimate concept of God, but fails to reach a decision, and so suspends belief. The discussion, Flew asserts, should begin from the presumption of atheism in the sense that any conception of God to be entertained must first be justified by the theist and that he must further provide sufficient reason for believing that this conception has application.[1] If we accept these distinctions we shall recognize four kinds of atheism (a) Cartesian doubt, (b) Agnosticism (in Flew's sense), (c) the atheism which declines to entertain any concept of God and (d) the explicit denial of God's existence on the alleged ground of established knowledge.

In the following discussion I think I have accepted Flew's challenge. The atheists I criticize are of the fourth variety, not those adopting the attitude that Flew recommends. They deny the existence of a God whom they somehow conceive, without considering whether it is a justifiable conception or even the one adopted by the theist. My criticism proceeds from their presuppositions, examines their validity, and develops their consequences.

On the other side, my own positive contention about God is preceded by an attempt to construct and justify an acceptable concept of the adequate object of worship and to give sufficient reasons for believing not only that it has application as a contingent fact, but that it must 'have application'—or better that it is fundamental to all thought and judgement and the ground of any existence whatsoever—of *any* concept's legitimacy and the possibility of any concept's having application.

The onus which Professor Flew places on the theist I have assumed and it is now the turn of the atheist to show whether and how he considers that I have failed.

The first draft of this essay was read by Sir Malcolm Knox, and I am much indebted to his comments and sympathetic criticism, for which I record my sincerest thanks. Without his warnings I should have made mistakes that would have marred the final product, and what appears here would not have had even such merit as it may now claim. I have also to thank Professor Andrew Reck, not only for the invitation to give the Matchette Lectures, but also for his efficient arrangements for the publication of the book, relieving me of those tedious negotiations that accompany any attempt in these times to get scholarly work into print.

[1] Anthony Flew, *The Presumption of Atheism and Other Essays* (New York, 1976), Ch I.

CHAPTER I

FAITH AND COUNTERFAITH

I

Theism is the belief in God. Agnosticism is the suspension of that belief on the ground of ignorance. Atheism is a claim to knowledge.

Believers and unbelievers alike have held that the existence of God cannot be demonstrated and many even esteem it piety and a virtue to believe without proof. Others allege that, even if the traditional proofs of God's existence are logically valid, they are compelling only for those who already believe. Kant argued that, though necessary existence might be involved in a definition of God as a perfect and infinite being, if the definition is rejected and disallowed and if the initial concepton is repudiated, no proof follows. It has been suggested (e.g. by R. G. Collingwood) that Anselm himself would have found this argument congenial. *Credere* was for him the prior condition of *intelligere*. Thus proof would rest upon belief, not belief on proof.

If a man declines to believe what he cannot prove and at the same time believes that no proof can be given of God's existence, he will not believe in God. But he will not on that account deny God's existence unless proof can be shown that there is no God; and that may well be as little forthcoming as its contrary. The atheist, therefore, makes a definite claim to know that God is a fiction without factual warrant; but if his thesis cannot be demonstrated, the claim is baseless, and atheism can be maintained only as a belief.

This is the first point that I am at pains to emphasize. If, without proof, God's existence can be asserted only on the strength of faith, the denial of God's existence is in no better case. Unless proof can be established for either thesis, we are confronted only with two rival creeds; and the adoption of either must somehow be justified. My aim in what follows is to examine the nature and grounds of such justification. It would be wrong, however, to rule out from the start the possibility that strict demonstration might be available one way or the other, and whether it is will be considered in the sequel. But if we begin from the common contention that God's existence is the object at best only of faith, we must ask on what grounds the denial of God's existence can be taken as anything more cogent.

This I propose to do first, examining in turn the claims made by each of the major atheistic figures in recent philosophy. The first question to be answered is whether firm grounds are produced by any of them for the denial of God's existence. If not, atheism is not knowledge but at best a belief alternative to theism. Nevertheless, it may yet be supported by argument. My second task, therefore, will be to examine the arguments offered by each of the philosophers who advocate atheism. Even if these be found wanting some case may be made for the critical force of these arguments and, in Chapter II, I shall assess their value as a cathartic of religious belief. Finally, I shall try to show that the positive alternative to religion which atheists advocate has implications that should carry them beyond the limits which they set for themselves and us. This will lead to a discussion of the reasons which have been and which may be given for adopting a theistic position and what form of theism might be rationally acceptable.

II

The proponents of atheism do indeed claim cogent grounds for their rejection of the belief in God. That their claim is to no less than established knowledge is evident from the writings of the more eminent among them. Nietzsche, for example, fulminates against belief itself, in the modern age, as unmitigated mendacity. 'Is there any difference whatever', he asks, 'between a lie and a conviction? . . . Every conviction has its history, its preliminary forms, its tentative shapes, its blunders; it *becomes* a conviction after not being one for a long time.

What? could the lie not be among these embryonic forms of conviction?' He goes on to identify conviction with partisanship and accordingly with distortion and mendacity. 'The priests', he continues, 'who are subtler in such things and understand very well the objection that can be raised to the concept of a conviction, that is to say mendaciousness on principle *because* serving a purpose, have taken over from the Jews the prudence of inserting the concept "God", "the will of God", "the revelation of God" in its place'.[1]

This quotation not only expresses Nietzsche's view but also exemplifies the style and level of his 'argument', which consists for the most part of invective and abuse: but it makes it indubitably clear that he does not regard his own atheism merely as belief. He explicitly asserts that it is based on knowledge. 'Our age *knows*', he declares:

'Even with the most modest claim to integrity one *must* know today that a theologian, a priest, a pope does not merely err in every sentence he speaks, he *lies*—that he is no longer free to lie "innocently", out of "ignorance". The priest knows as well as anyone that there is no longer any "God",[2] any "sinner", any "redeemer"—that "free will", "moral world order" are lies—intellectual seriousness, the profound self-overcoming of the intellect, no longer *permits* anyone *not* to know about these things . . . We know, our *conscience* knows today—*what* those sinister inventions of priest and Church are worth . . .'[3]

How we know is not explained, but that knowledge is the basis of denial and condemnation of religion is unmistakably the claim. As Nietzsche points his accusing finger primarily at man in the modern age we must assume that the knowledge he claims is scientific. It cannot be that modern man differs merely in temperament or aesthetic preference from the medi-

---

[1] *The Anti-Christ*, §55.

[2] The implication presumably is that at one time there was a God, which if God is taken to be an infinite and eternal being makes nonsense of Nietzsche's denial, and if he is taken to be some finite deity, makes it a denial of something that the theist does not assert.

[3] *Op. cit.*, §38.

aeval—for that would make atheism only an alternative prejudice. It is that he has access to superior knowledge, in contrast to earlier 'ignorance' and 'innocence'. And the claim is
made explicitly. Among the Ancients, Nietzsche asserts (with
justice), 'scientific *methods* were already there . . . the pre-
requisite for a cultural tradition, for a uniform science; natural
science, in concert with mathematics and mechanics, was on
the best possible road—the *sense of facts,* the last-developed and
most valuable of all the senses, had its schools and its tradition
already centuries old'.[1] All this he laments, was destroyed by
Christianity; but we today have won it back, he claims, 'with
an unspeakable amount of self-constraint'. In Nietzsche's view
Christianity is the natural enemy of science (the 'wisdom of the
world') and faith is a veto against it.[2] It is science therefore
that assures us of the death of God.

In Nietzsche's mouth this position is thoroughly inconsistent,
because, elsewhere, he is contemptuous of science[3] and he opts
for a complete irrationalism which would exclude all semblance
of science. He makes Zarathustra eulogize the clear sky, free
of all clouds and 'spider webs of reason'. 'Above all things',
he cries, 'stands the heaven of accident, the heaven of innocence,
the heaven of chance, the heaven of wantonness'.[4] This could be
taken as a protest merely against casuistry and logic-chopping,
but it is clear enough from Nietzsche's general attitude and his
antagonism to rule and order in this work[5] that his rejection
is of reason and purpose in the universe. 'Together we learned
. . . to smile uncloudedly down from bright eyes and from
miles distant, when below us compulsion and purpose and
guilt befog like rain.'[6] Moreover, the identification of purpose
with reason is correct, for purpose is the realization of design
and system which is the essence of reason. So Nietzsche con-

[1] *Op. cit.,* §59.
[2] Cf. *Op. cit.,* §47.
[3] Cf. *Beyond Good and Evil,* Pt. I, 12–14.
[4] *Also Sprach Zarathustra,* III, iv 'Vor Sonnenaufgang'.
[5] Contradicted by implication in *The Anti-Christ* by his castigation of
Christianity as anarchy. See *The Anti-Christ,* §58.
[6] *Also Sprach Zarathustra,* loc cit. I shall return to the theme of compulsion in the following chapter.

cludes: 'with all things, one is impossible—rationality' (ibid.). Chance is absolute freedom and prevails everywhere.[1]

Science by its very nature is the endeavour to explain rationally; that is, to reveal phenomena as ordered in an intelligible system. Without rationality system is impossible. Although some have maintained that contemporary quantum physics testifies to the prevalence in nature of random activity, this is by no means the only interpretation which the theory will bear (and is rather a perverse one). Much depends upon whether one locates the indeterminacy in the physical reality or in our knowledge of it. Even if we were to concede evidence of randomness at elementary physical levels, recognition of system and organization by every scientific account of higher stages, in the atom, in the molecule, in the crystal and in protoplasm is inescapable. Moreover, even in the realm of quantum physics the scientist, by the use of mathematics, seeks to give a rational account of phenomena arising from what is interpreted as random occurrence. It makes no sense, therefore, to reject rationality and then to exclude belief in God on scientific grounds.

Nietzsche's denial of God must be seen as (what it is) the rejection at once of rationality and science. But in that case it cannot be supported by reason and must be taken as a mere expression of feeling and conviction, which Nietzsche himself has identified with lying.

Let us, however, ignore the professed irrationalism and consider only the allegation that natural science gives us assured knowledge that any belief in God must be false. Immediately it must be acknowledged that no empirical science makes any such claim. On the contrary, many distinguished scientists have found belief in God quite compatible with their scientific theories, and many (like Albert Einstein and James Jeans)

[1] It is interesting to observe that for Descartes, God's will, being completely free and infinite, is inscrutable and unaccountable (Cf. *Meditations* IV). It is, accordingly, so far as man is concerned, equivalent to pure chance. It follows that strictly there is nothing to choose between Nietzsche's denial of God, with the enthronement of pure chance, and Descartes's affirmation of God's existence and inscrutable governance of the world.

have been more strongly inclined towards theism by reflection upon their scientific discoveries. How far theism gains support from science, or is compatible with it, we shall have to consider later more at length. Here we need only say that no special science, on scientific grounds, can legitimately pronounce, or ever has made claim to do so, on the question of the existence or non-existence of God.

If either affirmation or denial of God's existence is to be made intelligible, the first requirement is to make clear what is meant by the term God. And if that is a Supreme Being, creator and sustainer of the celestial and terrestrial scheme of things, neither the aim nor the result of any science is the establishment of its existence or non-existence. Natural science seeks to investigate only the general principles of order and interconnection of phenomena in nature. The ultimate presupposition underlying the existence of nature as a whole is not the subject matter of any special science, unless metaphysics is to be classified as such. The existence or non-existence of God is the object of religious belief and of metaphysical investigation. It is not a question upon which the natural sciences are competent to pronounce or ever seek to decide, and natural science has never claimed or could claim to prove, or to have produced cogent evidence for, the existence or the non-existence of a supreme originating and sustaining cause of the universe.[1]

Nietzsche lived in an age when confidence in the omniscience of physics had become somewhat overweening—a confidence that the best thinkers of the 20th century have lost. Laplace had recently declared, in answer to Napoleon's question, that God was a hypothesis of which his science had no need. But even he was neither so arrogant nor so dishonest as to claim that physics could demonstrate God's non-existence. Nor is that established by the disproof which science provides of many

---

[1] Cf. J. S. Mill (than whom it would be hard to find a more sceptical writer on religion): 'Science contains nothing repugnant to the supposition that every event which takes place results from the specific volition of the presiding Power provided that this power adheres in its particular volitions to general laws laid down by itself.' *Three Essays on Religion—Theism* (Longman, London, 1875), p. 136.

theories about the world, the heavens and the history of men, which have in the past been espoused by the Catholic Church and by the official institutions of other religions. It is not even true, as Nietzsche, in company with many others, alleged, that Christianity has been a constant enemy of science. The doctrines about the world which the early Christians and the Mediaeval Church adopted were the accepted scientific theories of the day, and their supersession by more advanced theories was initially opposed as much by scientists, for scientific reasons, as it was by churchmen. Science is of its own nature conservative, and new theories always meet strong opposition, often despite considerable empirical support. If it were not so their eventual acceptance would be unscientific, for they would not have withstood the test of criticism and meticulous investigation. In short, Nietzsche's announcement of the death of God (whatever it could intelligibly be taken to mean) is at best an expression of his own conviction founded upon no scientific or historical evidence and offered upon no rational grounds.

Marx and Engels, being less romantic and better acquainted with science, are on firmer ground than Nietzsche. For them atheism follows as a direct corollary from materialism, on the basis of which they explain away religion as ideology, in psychological terms. It is materialism that they assume to be established by science, the realm of hard fact empirically grounded. This position is simply assumed by both Marx and Engels, neither of whom makes any attempt to prove or argue for it.

In an early essay on 'Private Property and Communism', Marx (following Feuerbach) asserts that sense-perception is the basis of natural science[1] and that sensuousness establishes 'objectivity'. In his 'Critique of Hegelian Dialectic and Philosophy', he says that 'real, corporeal *man,* man with his feet firmly on the solid ground'[2] establishes his essential objectivity in relation to objects outside of himself, which are sensuous.

'To say that man is a *corporeal,* living, real, sensuous,

[1] *Vide Economic and Philosophic Manuscripts,* Ed. D. J. Struik, (International Publishers, New York, 1964), p. 143.
[2] *Ibid.,* pp. 180–181.

objective being full of natural vigour is to say that he has real, sensuous, objects as objects of his being . . .' (loc. cit.).

It is thus sensuousness that establishes objectivity and founds science. Marx here calls his view 'naturalism' and distinguishes it from both idealism and materialism, but just how it differs from the latter is not set out—presumably it is that 'naturalism' is made to depend on man's 'objectivity' in his awareness of the world of natural objects. But this is 'real, corporeal man . . . with his feet firmly on the solid ground', that is, material embodied man on a material ground amid material natural objects. Whatever is to be said of sensuousness as a mark of objectivity and materiality, or of sense-perception as the basis of science, the solid materiality of man and of nature is merely accepted on a common sense level, without any attempt at epistemological or metaphysical analysis such as is undertaken by Hegel, the idealist whom Marx is criticizing. No philosophical or scientific ground is given for the assumption that materiality exhausts the real and no explanation of what constitutes materiality.

Engels, in his *Dialectics of Nature,* sets out, with admirable clarity, an interesting evolutionary world-picture, but it is speculative rather than scientific (in any accepted sense), and from the outset he assumes materialism which he never demonstrates. Engels apparently believes that materialism is established by the fact that life emerged from inorganic matter and continued to evolve to human form—a process which he held to be cyclical over vast aeons. But even in our own day scientists have not yet established the evolution of living from non-living matter, although they assume it on weighty evidence, and the cyclical course of evolution is pure speculation.

In fact, materialism is not a scientific theory at all. It is a metaphysic, which at different periods in the history of philosophy, has been repeatedly adopted by thinkers. It may, from time to time (like many other metaphysical theories) have given impetus to scientific discovery; but it cannot be demonstrated either by empirical evidence or by deduction from self-evident principles. The existence of material things does reveal itself to sense-perception, but not matter as such. Still less can the non-existence of spiritual entities be empirically revealed. That all reality is material can still less be proved mathematically or by any purely deductive argument, and not even philosophers have ever attempted such proof.

Marx and Engels quite rightly trace back the materialist philosophy of modern times to the Cartesian dualism of thought and extension. They allege that this antithesis separated the physical, as the subject-matter of the empirical and mathematical sciences, from the mind and whatever pertains to thought, as the subject-matter of metaphysics. Their error is to obscure the fact that the whole diremption is the work of metaphysics, which equally faces the task of reconciling the opposites, and that materialism is but one way of doing so. They discount the correlative idealism simply by giving preference to the philosophical arguments advanced by those who developed one side of the dichotomy at the expense of the other.

The dualism itself was the product of the Copernican revolution in cosmology which required a mechanistic account to be given of the movement of the heavenly bodies and extruded mind from the physical world. Newtonian science which developed this requirement and dominated European thought throughout the eighteenth and nineteenth centuries, for this reason gave some pretext to philosophers for adopting a materialist metaphysic. It conceived matter as made up of irreducible, hard, particles and all motion as the result of mechanical forces. Now, however, the mechanism and atomism of Newtonian science is a thing of the past, and in the 20th century, science gives less pretext for adopting a materialist metaphysic than in any previous period. Atoms, once thought to be indivisible hard pellets of matter, have nowadays been resolved into complex structures of elementary particles each of which behaves like a complexification of energy. Matter is represented in relativity physics as a very high degree of curvature in space-time. For Quantum Theory, elementary particles, and waves of radiant energy behave in complementary ways and no material medium is found in which they can occur. They have been called 'waves of probability'. Neither matter nor energy can, today, be adequately represented by scientists except in abstract mathematical formulae. Accordingly, philosophical materialism can derive little support at the present time from any accepted scientific theory.

Nothing however follows from any of this as to the existence or non-existence of God. Equally, even if we were to assume the truth of materialism with Marx and Engels, neither atheism nor theism results. Many early versions of the latter are quite compatible with materialism, for in many religions of the past God has been imagined as a material being. And even if all matter were a manifestation of some immaterial entity, it is not obvious that it must necessarily be God. We have to conclude, therefore, that atheism is not a matter of knowledge even as professed by Marx and Engels, but only a presupposition, a matter of belief.

Freud displays a similar unquestioning confidence that all religious doctrine is illusion. Like Marx and Engels he bases his assurance on science, in particular the science of psychology. He assumes without argument or demonstration that the scientific investigation of nature of itself removes grounds for religious beliefs. Indeed it could be shown, though he does not show it, that this is the case with some religious beliefs, but it does not follow that it is so with all of them. In particular, belief in God, as we have seen, is neither established nor disproved by science, and Freud's conviction rests only on his psychological research. But whatever we may be able to learn from science about the psychological causes of religious attitudes and practices, psychology cannot reveal to us the truth or falsity of religious beliefs and doctrines, particularly it can tell us nothing concerning that of the assertion, 'God exists'. For that we must seek evidence in the nature of reality, not merely in the workings of the human mind. The contrary assertion, then, can only be made on conviction, is still only an expression of belief and not of knowledge.

If empirical science provides no proof of the atheist's contention it might still be maintained on philosophical grounds either Empiricist or Existentialist. The first of these is represented by Findlay's so-called Ontological Disproof, to which we may give some brief attention. The proofs of God's existence set out by traditional theism have been countered by Empiricism for the most part by demonstrations claiming to show their logical invalidity but at least one attempt has been made to go further and to prove the contradictory thesis. J. N. Findlay in *Mind* (April, 1948) argued that modern logic allows necessary propositions only to be analytic, and any assertion of existence is synthetic. It is, therefore, logically impossible for any being to exist necessarily. But necessary existence is the essential character of God, for no contingent being is adequate to the demands of the religious consciousness. Accordingly, the very conception and definition of God as a necessarily existent being is logically contradictory and his existence is impossible.

Unfortunately, the modern logical doctrine which underlies this proof by the same principle undermines it. For its conclusion states that the existence of God is a logical impossibility. According to the doctrine, however, logical impossibility, the negative form of logical necessity, can only be purely analytic, whereas the denial of God's existence is a synthetic proposition. If we adopt this view of logic we cannot prove by logic alone, and independently of empirical evidence, any factual assertion. And the assertion of God's non-existence is just as much a factual statement as that of his existence. Consequently, it should not be possible to prove either statement *a priori,* and again we may insist that atheism is, for the Empiricist, at best, an expression of belief.[1]

Jean Paul Sartre treats with disdain efforts to disprove the existence of God by formal logic. They are, he maintains, a waste of time, and their outcome could make no difference to the condition of man, whose acceptance or rejection of them can only be a matter of his own free and unrestricted choice. Such choice, for Sartre, is wholly independent of any rational consideration and is prior to all reasoning. Setting aside the implicit scepticism of this doctrine, for the moment, let us briefly consider the basis on which Sartre maintains the doctrine.

He takes more or less as an axiom the statement that existence

[1] I have dealt more at length and in greater detail with Findlay's disproof in *Revelation Through Reason,* pp. 57–63.

is prior to essence, which is held to imply that man has no 'nature' but what he himself creates by his own choice. In order to choose he must first exist. If there were a God on whom man's existence depended, essence would precede existence, for God must conceive man in order to create him, and so must preordain his nature as well as his existence, But as man is free, existence must precede essence, and there can be no God.

The implication is that, if there were a God, man could not be free; but that does not follow if God, as the tradition holds, gave man freedom. Nor is the possibility excluded that existence and essence are, in God, identical, and that it is precisely in such identity that complete freedom consists. For then freedom would not be a merely negative indeterminism, leaving all choice (whether God's or man's) purely arbitrary, but a positive capacity of self-determination, which would belong to God without qualification, and to man in an appropriate degree. Sartre fails to show that this is not the case, his own contention about the priority of existence to essence being dogmatic and unsupported. Of course one must exist in order to choose; but equally, if one is to be able to choose, one must be of such a nature as to have that capacity—essence as well as existence is prior to choice. Moreover, no man is free arbitrarily to accept or reject the proofs of God's existence unless he renounces rationality; and if he does that Sartre's own argument can have no significance for him. If arguments are at all to be considered, it must be rationally on their merits and with respect to their validity; and this will apply equally both to the traditional proofs of God's existence and to Sartre's reasoning from the alleged priority of existence to essence to the non-existence of a creator God.

The allegation of priority to essence of existence is, however, incoherent. Whatever exists must be some *what*. That which has no character or essence is nothing—and nothing does not exist. Sartre either ignores or fails to appreciate the truth of Parmenides' dictum; 'That which is not, is not', and likewise Plato's development of it in the *Sophist,* which established the

positive significance of negation. Sartre's own treatment of
negation in *Being and Nothingness* is tortuous and hardly cogent.
He fails to grasp and seems to misinterpret Hegel's theory,
which he discusses, apparently confusing concrete being, the
Absolute, with abstract being. It is the latter and not the
former that Hegel identifies with abstract non-being. Sartre
also fails to appreciate Hegel's conception (and its consequences)
of the immanence of the Absolute in all abstract categories.
Nobody who properly grasps the significance of negation can
allege that nothingness has independent reality. Obviously, if
it had, it would not be mere nothingness. Yet again, if it had,
it would, *per impossibile,* be some *what,* and so have essence.
The same must be true of existence, which as Hegel clearly
saw, is the manifestation of essence in actuality. Pure abstract
being is only implicitly actual, and as such is purely immediate.
Qua immediate, it may be said to be prior (in some sense) to
essence; but immediate abstract being is, in Hegel's logic, the
first provisional definition not of human nature, but of the
Absolute.

The existence which Sartre takes to be prior to essence is
finite existence; and that, to be anything at all, must be determinate. Indeed it involves negation (as Sartre apparently
acknowledges)—not bare negation, but significant negation involving an equally determinate other. But all this is much
lower in the dialectical scale than the nature or essence of
human consciousness and personality, which involves explicit
distinction and awareness of both self and other as object.
This too Sartre appears to realize, though not what it commits
him to. Consciousness implies the self-mediation of existence
as being-for-self, and is therefore explicitly essence and existence
mutually reflected and amalgamated in unified distinction. Freedom is this self-mediation in self-awareness, which cannot be
identified (incredibly) with nothingness, as it is by Sartre, but
is the premonition of a self-determined totality which transcends
the determinate limits of finite consciousness. We shall revert
and attend to this transcendence later. What we must here
affirm is that the priority of existence to essence assures freedom

only if existence is absolute and freedom the self-determination of essence through the immanence in it of an absolute subjectivity. The corollary of this implication is not the non-existence of God, as Sartre maintains; on the contrary, the being of God is what it reveals.

It is only because Sartre conceives freedom as arbitrary indetermination that he can identify it with nothingness and so taint consciousness with inanity; and only so would it seem plausible that the non-existence of God should be its condition. In sober truth, freedom is God's prerogative alone, and it pertains to man only so far as human self-awareness prefigures that absolute subjectivity which is infinitely self-determining. In the words of the religious tradition, man is free because he is created in the image of God.

Sartre's argument would have been sounder if he had moved from free choice to consciousness as its indispensable condition. To choose one must of course, exist; but choice, as opposed to mere reaction, involves awareness of what one is about. Choice implies consciousness, and in the last resort, choice that is truly free is inconceivable without deliberate thought. It is intelligence that most specifically distinguishes man from lower nature as fully human; and, in consequence, one may well conclude that, if man is free to choose, it is only because his intellect is his essence. Accordingly, whether or not we wish to maintain that existence is prior to essence, what we must assert is that intelligence, as essential to man's nature, is prior to his freedom of choice. Then whatever is implicit in self-reflective intelligence will be involved in human freedom, and that, we shall shortly find, carries us inevitably beyond the limits which all forms of atheism seek to impose upon our conception of the real.

III

If faith produces theism, then atheism may be called the expression of a counter-faith. But without some rational underpinning neither would be more than psychological states, irrelevant to any claim to truth, and we must therefore consider further the arguments advanced in support of each thesis if we are to judge responsibly between them. I shall do this as before, examining first the reasonings of the major proponents of atheism.

At the outset we must clear away one very prevalent confusion. There are two forms of it, but the confusion in each aspect is of the same kind. First, moral reprobation on the part of adherents and officials of institutional religions is entirely irrelevant to the truth or falsity of theism. Secondly, the absurdity, inconsistency, or untenability of doctrines taught and held by the orthodox in any organized religion does not necessarily affect the issue. Whatever Roman Catholic, Greek Orthodox or Protestant theology may prescribe, or the theology of any other religion, either now or in the past, the truth about the nature and existence of God is an independent matter and is neither established nor discredited simply by the official proclamation of any particular religious organization. Similarly it is neither established nor discredited by the criticism of special doctrines apart from the simple belief in God. What can be rationally established will naturally validate or invalidate particular religious doctrines. But atheism gains no credibility either from attacks upon the misdeeds of their followers, or from the implausibility of special dogmas, like virgin birth, holy trinity, or eternal damnation of the wicked. Even less is criticism of historical policies of any church relevant to the issue of theism versus atheism, like the oft and erroneously asserted hostility of the Papacy to science, or the one-time opposition of some protestant sects to the theory of evolution. Once this sort of confusion is recognized whole volumes polemic against established historical religions fall away (however well merited they may be) as arguments in favour of atheism, and a large part of the attacks both of Nietzsche and of Marx are seen to fall beside the main point.[1]

Nietzsche does not argue. He declaims, dogmatizes and vituperates. He is at one moment naturalist, at another pantheist;

[1] As do many of those offered by John Stuart Mill, Bertrand Russell, and others more recent. Cf. J. S. Mill, *The Nature and Utility of Religion* and *Theism;* B. Russell, *Why I Am Not A Christian.*

now romantic, now cynic; in one passage he is moralistic, identifying morality as the 'the expression of the conditions under which a nation lives and grows', in another he is immoralist decrying conventional virtues, especially compassion, and seeming to aggrandize revenge, malice and wrath. He apparently embraces a vague and incoherent evolutionism, which he does not elucidate, and he acclaims strength and nobility which he never defines or exemplifies. He idealizes a tribal god, vengeful and violent, and despises the good, the loving and the meek. Hence Christianity is vilified as decadent, and ultimately all belief is condemned as fraudulent. Presumably we are to be persuaded by this protracted diatribe that God is dead, no precise meaning ever having been assigned to the phrase.

Just what are we to understand by this declaration? Is it that the widespread belief in God hitherto professed is no longer entertained? As a general statement that would be patently false and Nietzsche does not himself assert it. Does it mean simply that there is no God? But if so, how could he have died? Are we to take it that God once did exist but has ceased to be? What sort of god could that be other than some idol which all genuine theists would reject? Or does the statement merely say that the old anthropomorphic conception of God is no longer viable? If so, of course, it does not rule out a more adequate conception and atheism is not entailed. To say merely (if that were the intention) that the issue is dead whether or not there is a God would be belied by the continuance of the debate. Perhaps we are to understand that belief in God is futile and ought to be abandoned, but then we have a right to demand reasons.

None of Nietzsche's polemic, however, unsupported as it is by argument, lends itself to philosophical discussion, nor does it merit serious consideration. Not even his *soi disant* historical interpretations can be soberly assessed, for they are not accompanied by evidence. One might well conclude, therefore, that Nietzsche's atheism is sheer prejudice requiring at best psychological explanation and giving no guidance as to the foundations of belief. But it would be too short a way with dissenters to dismiss Nietzsche's critique quite so easily, and we must look into it somewhat more closely. He is in fact trying to do for religion much what Marx and Freud did more coherently—that is, give a socio-psychological analysis of belief and religious practice. Through all his twisting inconsistencies and changes one may divine the thesis that religion, like philosophy, is a rationalization (false and hypocritical), or a symbolic representation, of instinctive drives, masquerading as the pursuit of truth, in one case, and as the morality of love and piety in the other. Or else it is the will to power impelling the priestly class to domination, through superstitious deception, over the rabble; or else, and at the same time, the symbolic expression of the resentment of the slave mentality against a nobility which characterizes its masters and superiors; or a projection of the slave's own wish-fulfilment into a hereafter, expressed in terms of bogus spirituality.

Presumably, if all this *per impossibile* (for not all these contentions are mutually compatible) were true, we could affirm the non-existence of God and the illusory character of religious doctrine. But as the thesis is supported by no coherent or scientific reasoning nothing compels us to accept it, and even if it were scientifically supported (as we shall have to repeat in reference to Freud), the atheistic conclusion would not follow. For, however much my instinctive urges may engender illusory beliefs or bogus attitudes *in me,* the truth about the world, independent of my believing, is not thereby affected. My will to power, or resentment, or what have you, may delude me into the belief that God exists, but the cause of the delusion does not determine the reality which the belief purports to present. If I were to be persuaded that the earth revolved round the sun because I suffered an inherent horror of being static and immovable, that would not prove that the belief was false. The psychological cause of people's beliefs ensures neither their falsity nor their truth.

The critique of religion offered by Marx and Engels follows four interrelated lines of argument. First and fundamental is the socio-economic doctrine of economic determinism. Next, fol-

lowing from it, is the epistemological theory of ideology. This
gives rise to a psychological explanation, and all together form
the foundation of historical interpretation. In coherence and
systematic consistency this theory is far superior to Nietzsche's
though in its psychological phase it has something in common
both with Nietzsche and with Freud. In brief the argument is
that the paramount determining factor in human life, which is
essentially social, is economic. Material needs and their supply
are basic to all man's activities. The method of production
determines the structure of society and that again the consciousness of its members.

Consciousness is the product of life and material production,
not *vice versa,* and the forms of consciousness reflect, directly
or symbolically, the social and material forces determining men's
lives. These forms constitute the ideology of the society, its art,
religion, philosophy and morality. As the means of production
are the source of wealth and power, that section of society which
controls them is the ruling class, and other sections form subject
classes, which the former keeps under oppressive domination in
order to retain its hold on the means of production. But as the
economic techniques improve, largely through division of labour,
society becomes more complex and a strain develops between
productive methods and social structure, which leads to class
struggle and eventual revolution. Ideology is expressive both
of the attitude and policies of the dominant class and of the
perpetual struggle between classes, one product of this being
religious belief. In terms of this economic determinism Marx
and Engels interpret history, that of religion along with politics
and philosophy.

Religion is the creation of man. It is, says Marx, the reflex
in imagination of the real world.[1] Man's search for happiness
on earth finds psychological satisfaction in the fantasy of a
'superman' and a paradise in Heaven.[2] The distress of the
working class finds expression and relief in a psychological projection of its wish-fulfilment into another world, the illusory

[1] Cf. *Das Kapital,* Bk. I.
[2] Cf. *Critique of Hegel's Philosophy of Right.*

world of the spirit. Religion is thus the opium of the masses, a form of alienation, a longed for self-realization in illusion, which makes the lot of the oppressed classes seem endurable and so is fostered and administered by the oppressors.

This is one Marxist account of religion. Another, not obviously consistent with it, is given in *German Ideology* and in Engels' critique of Dühring. Here we are told that man projects his fears rather than his longings. In the effort to supply his material needs and secure the objects of his desires man persistently strives to overcome and control the forces of nature to which he is subject. What he cannot control he personifies in the form of gods and hostile spirits, and as his control over nature increases godhead is transferred from the natural to the social forces which dominate his life. Again, in the *Communist Manifesto* Marx and Engels tell us that religion is merely the reflection of the thinking of the dominant class, rather than the wish-fulfilment of the workers, and the Mediaeval Church is said to have represented the feudal rulers against whom first the bourgeoisie revolted in the Reformation and secondly the peasants in their revolt in Germany, which Marx and Engels assert was betrayed by Luther.

How far these various accounts of religion agree together need not, for the moment, concern us. What is common to all of them is the doctrine that religion is part of an ideology, a sublimation as a form of consciousness of economic and social structures determined at base by material conditions. In all of them the objects of worship are taken to be illusory. It is by turning men's minds away from the illusions of Heaven, according to Marx, that we release them from the accompanying illusion of themselves as *Unmensch* on earth, and by abolishing religion, we can establish a philosophy of the real in this world. Like Nietzsche's, Marx's protest is against other-worldliness at the expense of the natural and the earthly; and the Marxian objective is essentially practical to prevent distraction by the myths and fantasies of religion from the exigencies of social reform in this world.

To the positive aspects of this teaching I shall return. What we are here considering is its denials. The adverse critique of other-worldliness and the hypocritical use of religion for political ends is welcome, as the sociological insight is often profound. Corrupt religion is on no account defensible. But the disproof of theism is not accomplished by the exposure of corruption in existing religions, and all that appears incompatible with theism in Marx's teaching is his materialism and that is compromised by his professed dialectic.

What theism asserts is that the ultimate reality transcends the finite, not that it excludes it. Marx's protest against this exclusion is, therefore, apt but not in itself atheistic. His denial of transcendence is what constitutes his atheism, but he and Engels both propound a dialectic, derived from Hegel, as the principle of development from the merely physical to the living and intelligent. Now mere matter which is purely physical remains unmitigatedly material and cannot evolve into life and mind simply by mechanical action. Materialism proper is committed to *reduce* life and mind to physics—a reduction which no science or philosophy has ever accomplished. Marx and Engels do not even profess to have done this. On the contrary they appeal to dialectic to bring about a process which moves in the opposite direction and produces consciousness from living and material structures. They give no adequate explication of the dialectical principle, except to say that it works through synthesis of oppositions; and how mere matter can do that is never explained. Hegel's account of dialectic is teleological and so consistently makes its product (Spirit) its determining principle; and Marx, while for this reason he accuses Hegel of standing on his head, does not explain how dialectic could work otherwise. In fact, by adopting an evolutionary principle, despite its professed materialism, the Marxist dialectic of nature[1] is crypto-teleological.

To be a strictly consistent materialist Marx ought to have maintained that consciousness was purely epiphenomenal and that it could have no effect whatever on material processes, whether physical, biological or social, and that would ill have

[1] Cf. Engels *Dialectic of Nature*.

consorted with his practical recommendations. But he explicitly denies epiphenomenalism and maintains only that economic conditions are the most important and the predominant influences on social change, never that conscious human efforts are inefficacious. Nor could he have done otherwise, for material needs are rooted in the processes of life; living impulse, to be living, must be felt; and human desire, to be desire, must be conscious. Without these one cannot intelligibly talk of human needs and their satisfaction, whether material or other. Similarly, without intelligence there can be no co-operative economic activity and no social structure. Thus the economic conditions which mould society are themselves conditioned by human thinking and awareness. Marx allows this, admitting tacitly that human intelligence is superior to instinctive and purely inorganic forms of activity.

The dialectic, therefore, is inevitably progressive towards higher forms of being and, if these are to emerge, they must be potential in its beginnings. If so, matter is not *mere* matter, but holds within its nature a principle of self-transcendence. That precisely is what the dialectic guarantees. Does it terminate in human social consciousness? Marx would say that it did, but can he do so consistently? This is what we must later investigate. Meanwhile, we can confidently assert that unless it can be shown that humanism necessarily excludes the self-transcendence of the finite, in human consciousness and elsewhere in nature, atheism cannot maintain itself on the basis of dialectic. This question will engage our attention in the following chapters but before I turn to it I must give some attention to the atheism of Freud and his psycho-analysis of religious consciousness.

As a psychologist Freud commands our respect and his psychological theories are not the object of my criticism—I claim no competence to judge them. But his writings on religion are philosophical not scientific, and, even if we assume that the psychological theories are sound, the philosophy based on them is incoherent.

According to Freud religion is a sort of infantile neurosis

stemming from the Oedipus complex, and one which he thinks it possible and desirable for civilized man to outgrow. Its manifestations are many and complex and I cannot enter here into all the convolutions and conflicts of Freud's explanation of the phenomena that issue from mental conflict and emotional ambiguity. The general outcome, however, is to the effect that religious belief is an illusion—not merely a theoretical or cognitive error—but an illusion born of repressed desire and fantastic wish-fulfilment.

The central doctrine in Freud's account of religion is that of the Oedipus complex, a state of emotional ambiguity in the son towards his father whom he at once loves, admires and tries to emulate, and jealously hates because of his sexual relationship to his mother. Physical fear combined with the natural positive emotions towards the father repress the negative impulses. There is thus a desire to kill and replace the father which is repressed and which is accompanied, in consequence of the operative fear and admiration, by a sense of guilt.

This general psychological analysis is read back into the pre-history of primitive man as he emerges from the animal level. Freud accepts from Darwin the suggestion that early man was gregarious, and, like other gregarious animals, lived in packs or 'hordes' consisting mainly of females and juveniles dominated by a single male. The leader of the horde was the mate of the females and the father of the children in the group. As the young males matured, they banded together against the father, killed and ate him, and then set up a fraternal society governed by the psychological urges, conflicts, repressions, compensations and defence mechanisms resulting from this primordial gruesome act of parricide. The guilt and remorse leads to ritual mourning, the fear to a projection of the paternal spirit as a father God, with further ritual practices to placate his ghost and expiate the original crime. These are the alleged sources of taboos and prohibitions, including self-protective rules against fratricide and, as a preventive measure against repetition, prohibition of incest. These are held to be the root origins of morality and religion and the beginnings from which social order developed.

This is a very brief and sketchy outline of a highly complex doctrine, which Freud elaborates in great detail in such works as *Totem and Taboo, Moses and Monotheism, Obsessive Actions and Religious Practices,* and *The Future of an Illusion.* In these and other writings Freud gives several different psychological explanations of religious beliefs and behaviour. They are perhaps not mutually incompatible, and in any case Freud covers himself with the assertion that religious phenomena are over-determined. Complex and diverse as the explanations are he maintains consistently that the Oedipus complex is central.

The fabrication of spirits and gods in imagination is attributed to the infantile tendency to personify inimical forces as the dreaded father. So primitive man imagines father-figure gods in natural forces. But as he comes to control these he transfers his personifications to social forces. (This doctrine comports with that of Marx and Engels.) Likewise early man projects his own ideas and cathexes on to the world, his repressed wishes and fears appearing to him as evil spirits, and these also embody the wrath, revenge and retribution of the original father (or, later, of dead relatives), combined with the survivors' own remorse and guilt feelings. So arises the idea of the soul from the sense of duality generated by the individual's own subconscious feelings and repressions. Taboos arise as psychological defence against temptations to indulge forbidden instincts, which, if permitted, would subvert social living. The forbidden acts are all associated one way or another with the primordial parricide and retribution for breaking the taboo is a ritual licence to other members of society to vent their own envy and fulfil their own repressed desires, either symbolically or actually.

The original parricide is expiated first by projecting the paternal presence on to a totem animal—another infantile trait —and the primary act of cannibalism is re-enacted in a sacrificial meal with the totem animal as sacrifice. This ritual identifies the participant in imagination with the sacrificial animal (as did the original cannibalism) and gives him its strength and virtue. So it effects a wish fulfilment. At a later stage the totem animal is relegated to an inferior status and the father-figure is revived as a deity, now both powerful and benign, as well as a jealous ruler and retributive judge. Still later the youthful descendants feel strong enough to elevate themselves into the father's place so the myth arises of the divine son, one with the father, who sacrifices himself for the sake of mankind and who is ritually eaten, as was the sacrificial animal in the earlier stage.

By and large, the beliefs are complicated wish-fulfilments—wishes to dominate, to enjoy sexual pleasures denied by elders, to obtain protection from external dangers, to retain the co-operation of others in securing the needs of life, to avert the envy and malice of neighbours, to placate one's own feelings of guilt without ultimately foregoing the actions which prompt them, and so forth. All this is a complex and elaborate form of infantilism and neurosis, which is corrigible by psycho-analysis and for which can be substituted, in healthy adult minds, a rational basis for civilized human living.

Now it can easily be shown that all this is, in various ways, unacceptable and incoherent. Let us begin with the anthropology. Darwin's suggestion, accepted by Freud, is at best speculative and there is no scientific evidence to support it, but if that consideration is waived it still fails to serve Freud's purpose. For among those animals which do live in the manner described the dominant male is not normally killed and eaten by a pack of his own offspring but, when he grows old and weak is challenged to single combat by one of the younger males and driven away into isolation more often than killed. Biologically it is necessary that single challenge rather than combined opposition should take place, because, if a pack of young males disposed of the patriarch, the leadership of the 'horde' would remain in dispute. Succession of leadership consequent on single combat would not have the psychological consequence alleged by Freud, the occurrence of which would, in any case, be doubtful at so primitive a stage of man's development.

Nevertheless, let us for argument's sake admit the biological assumptions of Freud's theory and concede that a band of brothers might have murdered their father and then have been overcome with remorse combined with fear of one another; let us suppose that they then develop the sort of neuroses and obsessions which Freud describes. How are these to be handed down from generation to generation and communicated to descendants who have not had the original experiences? Freud seems to assume a kind of universal social subconscious mind, for which evidence is not clearly forthcoming. No doubt all male offspring are liable to the Oedipus complex and possibly taboos and prohibitions psychologically motivated and socially enforced could arise out of it. But this could occur in any and every generation without assuming any original parricide. Conversely, a parricide might be committed without the alleged hereditary effects. To make the theory work we should have to presume the inheritance of acquired psychological characteristics, or else some equally implausible capacity among men for telepathic emotional communication. The psychological disturbances suffered by those who have murdered a parent are not necessarily or even plausibly transmitted to those who have not. And there are further, more serious difficulties to accepting Freud's doctrine.

That men should feel any sort of filial piety, such as could arouse a sense of guilt after violent opposition to a parent, presupposes an already developed moral sentiment reflecting an existing moral system. At the stage Freud envisages, not only is this improbable, it is actually assumed not to exist. For Freud makes morality the product of the psychological conflicts engendered by the primordial parricide, but the sort of conflicts requisite could arise only after moral ideas had already come into being. They are conflicts involving remorse for impiety which is not felt at the instinctual level. Fear and lust may well conflict, but that is not, and could not become, remorse or guilt unless it also involved moral disapproval of an act for which one held oneself responsible.[1] In fact, moral sentiments

---

[1] In *Civilization and its Discontents* Freud evinces an awareness of this *hysteron proteron* and even of the possibility that the whole story of the murder of the primaeval father might be mythical. But, somewhat typically, he extricates himself from the difficulty by attributing the sense of guilt to an original ambivalence—a conflict between Eros and the death instinct which will fit virtually any version of the facts one likes to produce, parricidal or pious.

can never be developed simply from instinctive feelings, because morality always involves self-awareness, reflection and judgment, without which emotional states of whatever kind have no moral significance. Morality, in short, is the product of reason and intelligence, which, though it transforms instinctual emotions and conflicts, cannot be derived from them alone. To imagine that it could be so derived is a fundamental ethical mistake of which Freud is not the only victim.

The view is more plausible that the child's image of his father as a protector against external dangers might be projected on to nature as an idea of God; and this image may well be associated with ambiguous emotions of fear and love; for the father is also an agent of punishment and an object of dread. But then the fantasy cannot be described exclusively as wish-fulfilment, as it would be equally a product of anxiety neurosis. Fear of God is no less a religious emotion than love of God. Wish fulfilment can then work either way, seeking comfort in the fantasy of a protective God or escape in the fantasy of a godless and indifferent nature.

Freud admits the possibility that scientific theories, including his own, could be wrong. But he does not seriously apply his own implicit epistemology to his own thinking. He castigates religious belief as a wish-fulfilling fantasy and classifies philosophical systems with paranoiac obsessions. He does not explain why scientific theories and psychological pseudo-philosophies should not be subject to the same strictures. Might Freud himself not be a victim of the Oedipus complex? Might not his infantile fear of a dominating father engender in him an anxiety neurosis which he projects in the image of a minatory God; and might he not then seek to suppress this terrifying image by denying God's existence and rationalizing his denial as a psychological theory? The ingenuity with which Freud turns all sociological and psychological evidence to the advantage of his own theory[1], and explains diverse or even contrary facts by means of the same Oedipus complex would give colour to the diagnosis of a paranoiac tendency in his own thinking. But I

[1] Cf. last footnote.

am not making this charge, I am pointing out only its plausibility and am appealing for consistency. Atheism, by the same reasoning as Freud uses, could as well be a wish-fulfilment fantasy as religion, with the same, or very similar emotional promptings.

Whether or not this is the case, and even if Freud's psychoanalysis of religious belief were sound and true, what bearing would that have on the truth or falsity of the proposition 'God exists'?—None whatsoever. Whatever prompts me to embrace a delusion makes no difference to the actual facts. If I or anybody else is to recognize it as a delusion we must know independently what those facts are, and must judge them by some objective criterion. Freud shows us how belief in God could be a fantastic wish-fulfilment, but if it is also illusory it can be so only because the facts differ from the fantasy. What objective evidence does Freud produce of that? None at all. He assumes that it is an obvious inference from the discoveries of science; but we have already shown that it is quite otherwise, and that no science provides any such evidence, least of all psychology.

Our conclusion, then, must be that atheism has no scientific grounding and is no less a matter of belief than theism. Moreover, the arguments advanced by its most eminent proponents are incoherent and unacceptable. At best, therefore, it has no stronger claim to credibility than any other faith. Nevertheless, it has performed a valuable cathartic function in the history of religious thinking the effect of which I shall recount in the next chapter.

CHAPTER II

THE POSITIVE FUNCTION OF ATHEISM

I

'Our age', wrote Immanuel Kant 'is indeed the age of criticism, to which everything must submit. Commonly religion seeks to exempt itself by virtue of its sanctity, and law by virtue of its majesty. But then they arouse justifiable suspicion against themselves and cannot claim that unfeigned respect which reason offers only to what has been able to withstand its free and open examination.'[1] Uncritical belief is unregenerate religion not far removed from bigotry. Only the religion that survives criticism is worthy of our reverence. Such criticism takes several different forms. Historical and textual examination of the scriptures is one of them; philosophical analysis of the objects and contents of belief and of religious concepts is another; scientific criticism of cosmological myths and allegations of miraculous events is a third, and moral criticism of religious practices and precepts is a fourth.

Atheism rests upon and embodies all these forms of criticism, and, in as much as it does so, it coincides with an essential element of developed religion. Disbelief of the incredible is an indispensable aspect of faith. For faith is, in the last resort, a belief in and devotion to an absolute truth (identified with God by St. Augustine), which will not tolerate uncritical acceptance of a dogma in conflict with other elements essential to our intellectual integrity. The dialogue in the soul, which raises questions and considers objections to every proffered thesis, involves a dialectic calling forth negation and opposition, of which, in the case of religion, atheism is the manifestation. If then atheism is no more than counterfaith and if the most notable arguments by which it has been supported are inconclusive or incoherent, it does not follow that atheism is valueless and is not an essential aspect of genuine religion.

[1] *Kritik der Reinen Vernunft*, Preface to the first edition, vi, n.

Not only is uncritical belief accompanied by the danger of bigotry, it may also become indistinguishable from superstition; and, apart from either of these defects, the most admirable and unshakable religious doctrine may, through long unquestioning acceptance, become complacent, lending itself to hypocrisy and pharisaism, a kind of lethargy from which it can be shaken only by violent and outspoken challenge. Religious practice whatever its merits, may become corrupt. Religious precept may be irreproachable, while the practice of its adherents may diverge lamentably from their profession, even when they believe themselves to be following it faithfully. The leaders of the Inquisition often sincerely imagined themselves to be following the behests of Christianity when they condemned heretics to the stake as if consigning them to Hell were an act of divine charity. Some of these deviations from the true path are independent of the actual validity of the religious creed; others may be the consequence of misconceptions and confusions within the doctrine itself. Exposure of such errors and corruptions is of unquestionable value, not only morally and for general enlightenment but for the cause of religion itself.[1]

II

The attitude of mind which accepts a religious creed without question, turns a blind eye to difficulties or inconsistencies, and countenances no critical examination, is what we call bigotry. Frequently (if not always) it is accompanied by intolerance, persecution, asceticism and repression (both of spontaneity in the individual and of disagreement in others). Against all this Nietzsche rails and fulminates:

'The Christian faith is from the beginning sacrifice: sacrifice of all freedom, all pride, all self-confidence of the spirit, at the same time enslavement and self-mockery, self-mutilation. There is cruelty and religious Phoenicianism in

[1] Cf. R. G. Collingwood, *Faith and Reason*. (Ed. L. Rubinoff, Chicago, 1968) p. 144: 'The defeat of superstition is a victory not only for reason but for faith too.'

this faith exacted of an over-ripe, manifold and much-indulged conscience. . .'[1]

If true, this would indeed be an indictment of the Christian faith, but with what confidence can we accept it from the mouth of one who, elsewhere, extols cruelty, selfishness and aggression and advocates hatred and strife.[2]

Bigotry with its accompanying symptoms is not, however, true religion, it is morbid religion. Accordingly, to seek some psychological explanation of it is apt and proper. To discern in it neurosis and obsession would not be surprising, or the rationalization of deep-seated unconscious interests and desires, whether prompted by instinctual urge or socio-economic conditioning. Against morbid religiosity the attacks of Nietzsche, Marx, and Freud are sound and salutary and are by no means irrelevant.

Another degenerate form of religious belief is superstition. A creed which is uncritically believed may nevertheless be true, or at least justifiable by possible argument. But belief contrary to evidence or good reason is mere superstition. That superstition and bigotry may overlap is obvious, for only the uncritical are likely to believe that to which evidence and reason run counter. To appeal to science to discredit outworn and obsolete doctrine is therefore legitimate and welcome. Engels does this systematically and effectively, Nietzsche with unconscionable inconsistency and Freud as a foregone conclusion. Irrational belief, moreover, can be explained only psychologically, and pathological promptings are often taken as the hall-marks of superstition. The thrust of the atheist's criticism is thus towards identification of all religion as superstition. But whether this assimilation is warranted is a further question and we must ask what precise creed falls victim to the strictures of such critics as those we have considered to find out whether this creed is what the most developed form of religion enjoins. If it is not, the identification of religion with superstition will not be justified.

[1] *Beyond Good and Evil*, III, 46.
[2] Cf. *Thus Spake Zarathustra*, I, Of Joy & Passion, Of War & Warriors, Of Friends; II, Of the Compassionate, Of three evils, Of Old and New Law-Tables, 10; IV, Of the Higher Men, 11.

That scientific demonstration can and does discredit many beliefs espoused by religious teachers is certainly the case, but this comes about not because religion and science are inherently in conflict. The contrary, we shall find, is the truth. It is because established religion, for various reasons, is even more conservative than established science, and when advances occur in knowledge, official religion which originally espoused earlier scientific theories, clings to them after they have become obsolete. It does not follow that religion cannot also develop and that more advanced scientific concepts must be incompatible with the essentials of religious faith. The function of atheism is to clear away the obsolete and rid us of superstition. Zarathustra's exultation in the clear sky and uncluttered conscience has genuine appeal, but we shall find it pointing more consistently to a new and purified theism rather than to atheistic nihilism.

It is widely admitted by theologians that the conception of God has changed and developed through the ages, and varies from one religion to another. Earlier ideas of deity are usually those that accompany obsolete views of the world such as typify superstition. Anthropomorphic images of God as a mighty and all-powerful king, a judge apportioning punishment and reward, the defender and protector of his people, were long ago prevalent and are today still entertained. To these characteristics is often added the notion of a magician who performs miracles with unlimited capacity. Any such notions are generally recognized today as the grossest superstition. That some such images may be used poetically and as an artistic medium through which to convey deeper truths is indeed possible, and we must always bear in mind that it is the most obtuse folly to mistake metaphor for literal statement of fact. But a writer like Nietzsche whose almost every line is metaphor and allegory can hardly be accused of that kind of stupidity. It is the literal acceptance of the metaphor by the devout believer against which protest is being made, but the protester must beware of the pitfall of concluding that the religious symbol stands for nothing whatsoever. With Nietzsche in mind we may observe in passing that the superstition which conceives God anthropomorphically creates the image of a super-*man,* and as Nietzsche's image of the *Übermensch* is never set out in detail we cannot tell how far it may be the same. It is perhaps significant that, in *The Antichrist,*[1] Nietzsche waxes nostalgic for the old Israelitish conception of God as the tribal deity—the God admired 'in good and bad alike,' a God of 'anger, revengefulness, envy, mockery, cunning, acts of violence,' knowing 'the rapturous *ardeurs* of victory and destruction.' But it is the critique, not the commendation, of superstition which is the valuable aspect of atheism.

That the primitive anthropomorphic conception of God is the target of Marx' and Freud's critique is clearly obvious. They both explain the development of the conception of God, beginning in primitive times as the personified forces of nature and society; and it is the later notion of a God set apart in a remote heaven, where our ultimate happiness is to be attained, against which Marx especially protests. This is the 'opium of the people' which distracts the attention of the workers from their oppression in this world by an idyllic picture of the next.[2] It is this superstition that projects into a world of fantasy the distress and alienation suffered in reality. Likewise, the products of neurosis and obsession which Freud describes, the wish-fulfilments and projections of guilt-feeling, culminate in the Father-figure who comforts and protects as well as punishes and rewards. All this, no doubt, is superstition apt to be explained away as the figments of imagination and psychotic illusion. But once these have been revealed for what they are, the board has not been swept clear of the legitimate objects of religious faith, to which we shall return in due course.

III

Next we have the atheist attack on the morality of religion, and here again the criticism is not always misplaced. It is this aspect which agitates Nietzsche the immoralist, most insistently, and his critique would be more helpful if his own conception of morality were not so defective and fluctuating that his criticism

[1] §16.
[2] Cf. *Critique of Hegel's Philosophy of Right.*

is largely lost in confusion. His main anathemas are hypocrisy and 'lies', neither of which, to be sure, are commendable. But castigation of the lie comes ill from one who, in the next breath commends falsehood, so long as it is used for an approved end[1] —an end, incidentally which he never clearly defines. Hypocrisy, moreover, implies recognition of genuine morality which is being feigned, but Nietzsche recognizes none. Condemnation of hypocrisy implies disapproval of the hidden motives of the hypocrite. According to Nietzsche, they are lust for power and resentment of its possession by others. These, however, are the very ends which elsewhere he extols. Can we wonder that Zarathustra repeatedly complains of the apostacy and inconstancy of his followers? Again, the morality of interdiction, repression and revenge moves Nietzsche to scorn and indignation, while he castigates Christianity in one breath as the religion of compassion and forgiveness, signs, he declares, of weakness and decrepitude, and in the next breath admires the revengeful, violent, warlike virtues of the ancient tribal Jehovah.

Morality is too complex a matter to be criticized or advocated in sweeping statements. Resentment and revenge are indeed reprehensible, but much will depend upon the nature of their objects. Resentment of injustice and retribution against violent crimes may be highly praiseworthy in defence of a just and humane society. Corruption and hypocrisy are certainly not to be tolerated, but they can be seen for what they are only in the light of clearly defined social and moral objectives. The relevance of all this as a critique of religious belief is that professed devotion may often serve as a cloak for evil and insincerity. When that occurs, the critique is an indictment of the perpetrators, but it is not, by that same token, a condemnation of religion.

'Lilies that fester smell far worse than weeds'. *Corruptio optimi pessima.*

Another defect of historical as well as contemporary religion has been blatant inconsistency between doctrine and practice. Christianity in particular has always preached love and for-

---

[1] Cf. *Anti-Christ,* §56 *et seq.*

giveness, charity and peace, while its professed adherents have, in its name, practised persecution and war and indulged in every conceivable form of vice and violence. But if we condemn the latter we *ipso facto* approve the former. Atheistic writers invariably attack these lamentable failures in the Christian Church. No doubt other religions suffer similar infidelity and inconsistency among their own professed advocates. And it is all much to be deplored. But we must not be misled into concluding that the thesis of atheism follows from it. Not only would that be logically *non sequitur,* but similar criticism, condemnation and castigation has been voiced by devout believers even more frequently and copiously than by those whose repulsion from the ill conduct of clerics has persuaded them to abandon religion. Savonarola was no atheist, nor was Martin Luther.

Nietzsche and Freud, as well as Marx, have made much of the use of religion for political purposes. Nietzsche alleges that Christianity, under the leadership of Paul, became the instrument for ensuring priestly power over the masses, as Judaism had been before it. He counters anti-semitism not by repudiating it or by defence of Judaism, but by a *tu quoque* to Christianity and an antisemitic attack on Paul.[1] Marx's argument is common knowledge. Religion is an ideological tool for maintaining the dominant position of the ruling class which controls the means of production.[2] Freud likewise sees religious taboos, psychoanalytically explicable, as reinforcing and maintaining the prohibitions requisite for the stability of civilized society. But it is a prop which, he feels, does at least as much harm as good in generating emotional conflicts, neuroses and frustration. He recommends its removal by psycho-analytic enlightenment and its replacement by an appeal (*mirabile dictu*) to the Logos of reason.[3]

Again we must admit, whether we take a Marxist view, a Freudian, or some other, that religion often has been, and may still today be, used as a political weapon. It may be openly ex-

[1] Cf. *Anti-Christ,* §§39–45.
[2] Cf. *The Communist Manifesto.*
[3] Cf. *The Future of an Illusion.*

ploited, or subtly infiltrated into the social order, or it may be a subconscious psychological motivation. But how does this fact bear upon the truth of its doctrine? If that is a false superstition, it is liable to do only harm, and, *pace* Nietzsche, few today will defend Plato's doctrine of 'the noble lie'.[1] On the other hand, if the religious teaching is true, or is a symbolic representation of the truth, its influence on society may be beneficial. We can say only 'may be', for the unscrupulous can always misuse sound doctrine for base ends. 'The Devil can cite Scripture for his purpose.' But the misuse of truth cannot, no more than its distortion, discredit the truth itself, and whether a religious belief is true or false cannot be decided according to the use made of it by political interests or social miscreants.

We may conclude, therefore, that the attacks launched by the atheist, though telling against malpractices in religion and against its social misuse, are beside the point in any discussion of its truth. His socio-psychological analyses of religious ritual and belief, though not in all cases scientific, may well be revealing and have monitory value, but they have no direct bearing upon the validity of the theist's argument.

IV

More important than the negative critique of atheism are its positive recommendations. All the critics offer alternatives to theism which are more than mere denials; and the implications of these affirmative prescriptions go beyond what their authors are prepared to tolerate. Inconsistency is a blemish of small concern to Nietzsche, as perhaps one might expect from a confessed (or should we say, half-confessed) irrationalist. In place of the supernatural he extols the Earth, in place of spirit he honours the body (though time and again he appeals nostalgically to *Geist*). But he finds man no sufficient substitute for God. Man he largely despises, especially in the mass; and Nietzsche demands that man be treated only as a transition,

---

[1] Cf. Nietzsche, *Anti-Christ* §56, and *The Use and Abuse of History*, in which Nietzsche himself advocated the noble lie. If Plato is rightly understood, however, the noble lie is not a lie at all.

seeking at best his own supersession by a new race of Superman. Thus self-sacrifice and altruism which, in Christian virtue, Nietzsche excoriates as sickness and debility, are replaced by the self-sacrifice and self-denial of the whole race, which must become a mere bridge to its own destruction (*Untergang*) in the generation of a superior race. How this doctrine consorts with Nietzsche's commendation at the same time of selfishness, power-lust, boldness and pugnacity we must leave for others to decide.

Just what the superiority of Superman consists in, we are not told any more than we are told how nobility and courage differ from the much reviled virtue and goodness. But let that pass. What we are offered is not humanism but superhumanism and how that differs from a kind of prospective mythology or from anthropomorphic deism projected into the future is left unexplained. But Nietzsche gives numerous indications that he is espousing some sort of evolutionism. Earth and body are to be honoured, Christian and conventional morality are deplored as 'harmful', presumably to the race, as counteracting natural selection and the survival of the fittest—the strong, the courageous and the enlightened self-seeker. This natural process of evolution, if encouraged and fostered would, we may assume, generate a new and better species, a Superman, the end of all desire and endeavour.

My main aim is not to reveal the self-stultification of this teaching, but its futility cannot be passed by in silence. If the evolutionary process were actual and merely natural, what need would it have of Nietzsche's exhortation? If Christian morality is 'harmful' it will lack survival value and be eliminated without the philosopher's condemnation. If man's folly is a misadaptation to environment he is in any case doomed and Superman must inevitably be in the pipeline. What need then of spending oneself devotedly in the service of one's own submersion for a future race the welfare of which one cannot share? But apart from need, what pretext or incentive could men have to follow Nietzsche's prescription other than some Freudian death-wish? What satisfaction did Archaeopteryx derive from the emergence

of the modern eagle? The only end for man that he has motive
to pursue is one in which his own will is realized, but he can
no more will the natural evolution of his own species than he
can add, by taking thought, a cubit to his own stature.

In spite of himself, Nietzsche is aware of this. The will to
power, he sees, is man's inevitable aim. The question, however,
arises: Power to do what? Power of what sort? Clearly not sheer
physical power, or elephants and horses would already be
man's superiors. The only power mankind finds worth his
aspiration is the power of the intellect, in which alone his
superiority consists. It is the power of intellect with its reflective
capacity which makes man human and places him above the
simple beast. 'All too human', growls the cynic, Nietzsche—
though in other moods intellect is his god and Pascal is reviled
for allowing Christianity to corrupt his intelligence. But again,
an aspiration to what transcends humanity can only be engendered through that same self-reflection which reveals men's
defects to themselves and to the philosopher who is himself
but man. Nothing but reason and self-consciousness could reveal
to us our own limitations; nor is any limitation revealed unless
and until it is surpassed. It is self-conscious intellect alone that
can conceive a good, without which superiority is meaningless
and superman a senseless shibboleth. Beyond good and evil lie,
at opposite poles, only better and worse. It is self-conscious intellect alone that can engender any recognition of the second,
or any aspiration towards the first which goes beyond the blind
instinctive urge. Mere feeling is inadequate to aspiration, and
hedonism itself, as a conscious quest, must become the infusion
of thought into instinct, which will drive it beyond itself and
will rest content in nothing limited to mere physical gratification.
And Nietzsche holds no truck with hedonism. Moreover it is
only through the power of his mind that he can exhort his
readers to seek the propagation of Superman. But Naturalism
never can, as we shall see anon, successfully explain the advent
of self-transcendent consciousness, and presents us ever with
a truncated image of human personality. Meanwhile, both
awareness of shortcoming and its attendant self-transcendence

implies an ultimate goal, a goal that Nietzsche, for all his bitter scorn and disavowals, never abandons. And that ultimate consummation conceived by mankind only in vague premonition, is what we call God.

Criticism of capitalism and bourgeois ideology far from exhausts the Marxian message. Capitalism, as we have all by this time learnt, is to be followed by socialism and Marx and Engels both herald and cry on the revolution. But the classless society which they advocate is not commended simply because it is historically inevitable and economically necessitated. Marx is well aware that all economic systems are designed to fulfil human needs; and it is not just the inefficiency and obsolescence of capitalism that he castigates, but essentially its injustice. Communism is promoted as liberation from oppression, alienation and exploitation, as the social order in which all men realize their potentialities and come into their own. Again, despite apparent cynicism and disavowal of sentimentality, Marx's chief motive is humanitarian. The aim of Communism is social justice to be achieved by equitable distribution of wealth, through mutual help and service to the community.[1]

However the Marxist may protest, he aims at a moral ideal, and his zeal is for the good of his fellowmen. In the revolution and the classless society he finds an end with an absolute claim upon his devotion—a moral imperative which rests on something far beyond the gratification of his own desires. No classless society or socialist system could rest firm on human selfishness alone and the Marxist condemnation of self-seeking in the capitalist is not for the sake of mere self-seeking among the proletariat. It is to be society, the commune, the group and not the individual whose welfare shall be the communist goal. Once again we have come upon a self-transcendent will and the conception of a goal which goes beyond the particular individual self.

---

[1] It is hardly insignificant that, for all its professed atheism, the Marxist slogan is culled from the Scriptures.

'If any would not work, neither shall he eat' is Paul's admonition to the Thessalonians.

That Marxism indispensably involves reflective reason cannot be denied. Not only is this true of the doctrine as a philosophy, which obviously requires the exercise of a reflective intellect. It is also implicated in the tenets of the theory. Economic organization of any kind is the fruit of human reflection upon men's needs and the material conditions of their life. Social structure consequent upon this is the product of human thinking. Its development, is dialectical: that is, it is a development in and through thought—a teleological development whose end is implicit in its beginnings. In its course human self-interest burgeons out into the interest of a community, and self-seeking, through self-reflection, becomes the quest for social justice. This is because human self-interest is never merely self-centered, because it is always self-reflective and so is aware of its dependence on the cooperation of others. Thus it inevitably transcends itself and seeks a larger end. The Marxist would say that, true though this may be, the end is just society and we need go no further. But there are other implications of the doctrine that still must be pursued.

The classless society is extolled as that which provides the conditions for the full development of human personal potentialities; and these are not limited to manual labour, however necessary and fulfilling even that may be. The capacity of the human mind is self-reflective and its nisus drives beyond the limits of the particular creature. Men, as we have said, are aware of their inter-dependence—that is, they are aware of themselves as members of a wider whole. The individual thus comes to identify his own realization with that of the group. But this process is self-propagating because no group is wholly self-sufficient and, so the objective must be progressively widened until all mankind is included. Again, material welfare serves wider interests just because our capacities are self-conscious and reflective. So once our physical requirements are met (and even sooner) we seek beauty in art, truth in science and philosophy, as well as satisfaction in mutual help and service. The complete fulfilment of these capacities cannot be restricted to economic production and distribution, which are means to that fulfilment not its end. And the end always transcends the finite particular, the endeavour is always towards a completion which lies beyond the merely finite.

The same implicit self-transcendence is to be found in Freudian teaching, when we examine closely the objectives that Freud offers. Let us suppose, for the moment, that Freud is right in his psycho-analysis of religion; that it is a kind of neurosis rooted in the Oedipus complex. Nevertheless, he maintains, it is equally the source and the support of social order. Civilization, he says, depends on the repression of certain instinctual drives and the consequent psychological defences, phantasies and projections aid and uphold the indispensable prohibitions. Civilization, moreover, is a commendable condition and it should be desirable to foster religion as its bastion. But this is not Freud's view. Mankind he thinks ought not to remain retarded in infantile neuroses but should become adult and should recognize the rational character of civilized life, the scientific facts of psychology and the reasoned basis of social order. Reason must be substituted for instinct and repression, and the Logos must take the place of the traditional God.[1]

In spite of his earlier protestations, it seems, Freud is not convinced that reason is quite incapable of overcoming psychological compulsions, nor is it always reducible to 'rationalization' of repressed cathexes. To hold that it was would, as we have seen, impugn his own theory. Not all systematic thinking can be dismissed, in the way that Freud dismisses philosophy, as paranoiac.[2] If it could, what would be the status of that thinking which recognizes paranoia as an ailment? Neurosis must be seen for what it is by a consciousness which itself is sane and one that is capable of self-reflection and self-criticism, one that is adult and mature, capable of detecting and liberating itself from infantile obsessions. It is truth that is the criterion both of itself and error, the same which judges both of itself and of derangement. Logos is the God Freud recommends, and in those terms; although, he says it is a God which works more

[1] *The Future of an Illusion*, §X.
[2] Cf. *Totem & Taboo* §III and *The Future of An Illusion* §VI.

slowly and patiently than the commonly imagined father-figure is permitted to do by his devotees. But truth is what Augustine identified as the God of the tradition, and St. John opens his Gospel with the declaration that 'In the beginning was the Word (Logos) and the Word was with God, and the Word was God.' Freud's atheism here looks uncommonly like theism.

The reason which is the foundation and sustaining mentor of civilization is not, presumably, the concoction and the plaything of the Id. It is not just a mirage playing upon the turbulent surface of repressed and conflicting emotional complexes. It is that which reflects upon all these and presides over them, reflects too upon itself and is aware of its own vulnerability to their assaults, as well as its own capacity to repulse and rise above them. Reason, moreover, in recognizing the weaknesses of the mind, the needs of the human organism and the dangers of unrestrained libidinal gratification, can regulate, direct and organize human conduct so as to make civilization possible. If it were not so, Freud's appeal for maturity of outlook and the substitution of Logos for neurotic illusion, would be an exercise in futility.

What then is this rational capacity to organize and regulate? Where does it originate, how and whence does it emerge to take control? Freud does not tell us. Possibly it has its roots far down in the nature of things. Biologists do find an analogous agency at work in living organisms and even physicists discern the workings, in the structure of matter, of organizing influences. Organization implies unity among a diversity of elements, and in organized wholes it is the totality that determines the elementary details. In the processes of genesis, the integrating principle is that which controls and directs. The explanatory principle is always that of structural integration and so always lies beyond the mere aggregation of the parts. It may well be that this tendency toward organized wholeness and integration in nature (about which I shall say more in the sequel) emerges in man as self-conscious reason; and that this is why reason, being the agency of order and unification, is that which rules and governs. Equally it is why reason is always teleological. What is teleological, however, we have already seen, holds within it the germ and principle of that which develops from it, and hence finds its explanation, and in a real sense its true being, in that by which it is transcended. The appeal to reason, therefore, is always an appeal to that which goes beyond the merely finite.

And this reason or Logos to which Freud finally has recourse is the one mental power for which his theory does not account. Not even the super-ego explains the whole character of self-reflection and critical assessment, the ability of the mind to examine, scientifically, dispassionately and uninfluenced by emotional impulses, the nature of its own subconscious disguises. For the super-ego is the identification of oneself in the first instance with one's parents, which results in early infancy from the Oedipus complex, and later one's self-identification with teachers and mentors, so that it imposes upon the self in mature life, the injunctions and prohibitions originally enforced by these feared and admired superiors. But how could such self-identification enable the super-ego to recognize itself as just that, and to analyse the personality over which it presides as the threefold structure of id, ego and super-ego? The psycho-analyst views the personality and pronounces his verdicts from above the super-ego; and what in psycho-analytic theory can account for his ability to do so? The nearest Freud comes to answering this question is to suggest that the energy for the work of thought itself may be supplied from sublimated erotic sources. Even if this is true it does not explain how thought comes to recognize itself as thus propelled, how libido can become aware of its own sublimation, of its alternations from Eros to death-instinct and of the super-imposition of ego upon id and super-ego upon ego. If psycho-analysis were the last word, psycho-analysis as rational scientific investigation would itself remain to be explained. Seeing itself for what it is, even in its unconscious depths, the self-conscious mind of man has here again transcended itself and has discovered a Logos which goes beyond everything that its own psychology can reveal.

V

In the first chapter I argued that atheism was as much a faith as theism, but a word may not come amiss about the relation of faith to knowledge. To believe something is obviously to believe that it is true, and in this respect knowledge and belief coincide for what one knows one necessarily believes to be true. The difference consists only in that knowledge demands explicit and adequate grounds, while belief may be harboured with insufficient evidence or none at all. But though we may believe without conclusive proof, we need not, therefore, be wholly irrational. There may still be good reasons for holding the conviction we adopt.

Man's awareness of himself and his encompassing world involves inevitably the propensity to grasp things in their mutual relation, as well as his own relation to others. Our practical necessities as well as our inveterate curiosity compel us to develop this relational structure of which we are aware and to push it to its utmost limits. Practical issues are not sufficient in themselves to determine what we shall believe; for practical success, and what it consists in, is itself a question that reflection must decide. Contentment and final satisfaction are not attainable short of intellectual comprehension, and practical life, if it appears to us to be 'meaningless' and ultimately futile (even though, for the moment, ostensibly pleasant) will fail to satisfy, and will not seem ultimately worth living. We have an ineradicable urge to seek ultimate explanation and to pursue understanding, and when we fail, we still entertain ideas in the light of which our present condition as well as our possible destiny appear intelligible to us. Accordingly, the justification of beliefs, whatever they may be, is always in the last resort, rational. It is always and only in terms of their explanatory efficacy that they can be rationally compared.

It is here that we reach the final criterion for the critique of atheism, or of theism. In the case of the former we find that it resolves itself into scientism, naturalism and humanism. But all of these doctrines are precluded from offering answers to ultimate questions. The origin of the universe, the ultimate nature of existence, the critical awareness of consciousness which makes science itself possible—these are all enigmas for science, and enigmas which it does not profess to elucidate. They can be tackled only by metaphysics, and when that has failed to resolve them finally, it has always pointed beyond the limits which atheism sets for man to an asymptote where the resolution must dwell.

Even science itself demands this transcendence for it cannot rest on its own base. It can give no complete explanation of anything, yet its fundamental presupposition is that everything is in principle completely explicable in rational terms. If it were not so the quest of science would be futile. Naturalism assumes the concept and accepts the fact (as who could not?) of Nature, but does not explain the possibility of either.

Humanism postulates the competence of self-conscious intellect as the chief characteristic of human kind, but can give no coherent naturalistic account of it. Attempts like Existentialism, to give a non-naturalistic account of humanity and to deny to man a human essence, at the same time assign one to him. The nature of man which Sartre denies he immediately replaces. Man's nature, he asserts in effect, is freedom, and freedom is choice, and choice is, or at least involves, consciousness—and consciousness is self-transcendent. Choice is unquestionably teleological, it seeks an end beyond the 'this' and the 'now'. It seeks a fulfilment which lies beyond its present status, a fulfilment which it cannot achieve in any finite, transitory object. Once more, it transcends itself. Humanism cannot be humanism without pointing beyond the merely human.

We must conclude therefore that atheism, in its very nature, and not only the examples we have examined, does not and cannot attain the explanatory goal at which it aims and on the presupposition of which it rests. God is denied and theism rejected as an unnecessary hypothesis. Explanation, it is alleged, is possible without appeal to what exceeds the bounds of nature or human reason. The denial thus depends upon the claim to explanatory power and is subject to the demands of reason. But the ultimate explanatory need is to transcend the finite understanding, which points beyond its own limits in its persistent effort to meet its own demands. Nature is not its own explanation. As Hegel declares, the question 'What is Nature?' is one which science cannot answer.[1] And reason, as we have seen, is inherently self-transcendent. Atheism, therefore, sets itself a task which it stops short of completing and a question to which its own answer is evidence of its insufficiency.

Even so inveterate a materialist and humanist as Feuerbach, in whose teaching Marx's atheism is founded, recognizes the self-transcendence of the finite in humanity and sees the essence of religion in that very fact.

'The essence of man, in contrast to the animal, (he writes), is not only the ground but the object of religion. But religion is the consciousness of the Infinite; it is thus, and can be no other than, man's consciousness of his own, and indeed not finite, limited, but infinite essence.'[2]

'Atheism', he asserts, 'is the secret of religion itself'.[3] More truly, he should have said that in atheism itself the secret of religion is concealed.

---

[1] Cf. Hegel's *Philosophy of Nature*, Tr. A. V. Miller (Oxford, 1970), p. 3.
[2] *Das Wesen des Christentums*, Ch. I.
[3] *Ibid.*, Preface to the Second Edition.

CHAPTER III

TRANSCENDENCE OF THE FINITE

I

The position we have so far reached is that belief in God, regarded as something less than fully established knowledge, is not confronted by any belief which can rightly make claim to established knowledge, but only by counter-faith. Atheism, however, serves the positive function of negative criticism. It serves to purge religion of superstition and to make us aware of bigotry and hypocrisy, as well as of inconsistencies between profession and practice. But such criticism of false and degenerate religion, does not demolish religion as such.It leaves open the possibility of a theism supported by reason and demanded by the intellect in search of ultimate explanation; as well as of a practical precept that may not be faulted even if it may often be violated. The purpose of this chapter is to examine that possibility.

The association of criticism, biblical and religious, with atheism is of long standing. Spinoza, who is unsparing in his condemnation of superstition, was reviled in his own day (and since), and hailed by Engels and Marx, as an atheist. But he himself repudiated the accusation most strenuously. His philosophy stands as evidence of the possibility of a theistic doctrine compatible with the rejection of all that the atheist finds objectionable. Spinoza holds no brief for superstition, but he distinguishes it clearly and sharply, as what he calls *religio vana,* from true religion—*religio vera.* Superstition he sees as the product of ignorance and the unrestrained flight of imagination, resulting in conflict of the emotions of hope and fear. Men give way to powerful desires which they find difficult or impossible to satisfy. Their aims are threatened by natural forces and conditions beyond their control, so they become a prey to fears alternating with unfounded hopes. In this state of insecurity they allow their imagination to contrive comforting beliefs—

the wish fulfilments of which Freud later came to speak—imagining irate spirits who demand placation and gods who reward adulation with capricious providence. The depths of inanity to which people are led in this way evoked Spinoza's contempt and ridicule: '. . . each,' he writes, 'has devised, according to his own bent, a different form of worshipping God, so that God might love him above others and direct all nature to the service of his blind cupidity and insatiable greed.' (*Ethics*, I, App.)

Anthropomorphism Spinoza rejects, not just as wishful thinking or anxiety neurosis, but also as logically incoherent, and inconsistent with any acceptable conception of an infinite deity. The scriptures he respects but refuses to take simply on authority. They are for him historical evidence of what constitutes prophecy and revelation, and this is itself to be discovered only by a rational and critical study of the sacred books. Miracles he rejects as contrary to God's nature, and appeal to them as an appeal to our ignorance which can reveal nothing of God and can provide no basis for faith. The butt of all this criticism is what atheism castigates, but Spinoza rests his critique upon a positive concept of deity, the implicit criterion involved in all criticism to which atheists are blind.

Nevertheless, Spinoza's denial of traditional beliefs about God and his ridicule of superstition, as much as his identification of God with Nature, brought upon him the accusation of atheism. Velthuysen wrote to Spinoza's friend Ostens: 'He has laboured more than enough to free his mind from every superstition. In attempting to show himself immune from it he has gone too far in the opposite direction, and . . . he seems to me to have cast off all religion.'[1] But Spinoza strenuously denied the charge. 'What he understands by religion', he replies, 'I do not know. Does he cast aside all religion, I ask, who maintains that God must be acknowledged as the highest good and that he must be loved as such with a free mind?'[2] Religion, Spinoza defines as 'Whatever we desire to do, of which we are the cause so far

[1] *Epistle* XLII.
[2] *Epistle* XLIII.

as we have an idea of God, or so far as we know God' (*Ethics* IV, xxxvii, S. 1). Atheism is the direct opposite of Spinoza's intention. He thought he could prove God's existence conclusively and when asked by Albert Burgh how he knew his philosophy to be the best, he replied 'I do not presume that I have found the best philosophy, but I know that I understand the true one. If you ask how I know this, I shall answer, in the same way as you know that the three angles of a triangle are equal to two right angles' (*Ep.* LXXVI.) What he denied were what he considered to be misconceptions about God, and his whole endeavour was to render intelligible and consistent the idea of God that traditional religion presupposed.

Atheists, for the most part, regard the inadequate notions of God which are current among believers as the only ones possible, and they deny, quite rightly, the existence of their objects. In this denial, Spinoza is at one with them. Such ideas, he holds, are products of the imagination and are mainly false. But that there is an adequate idea of God he is certain, and equally that the existence of its object is indubitable. I shall not enter, at this stage, into Spinoza's reasoning but will consider first one approach to belief that must be eschewed.

II

While Spinoza defines religion in terms of knowledge of God, the highest and most adequate knowledge, his older contemporary Blaise Pascal builds his argument for faith on the profundity of human ignorance. We know, he reminds us, only that 'life is but a moment; that the state of death is eternal, whatever may be its nature,' hence all our actions and thoughts must be affected by the nature of that eternity. 'It is impossible,' he writes, 'to take one step with sense and judgment, unless we regulate our course by the truth of that point which ought to be our ultimate end'.[1] Either God exists or he does not. Either there is an after-life or death is sheer annihilation. Which is the case reason cannot tell us, we are utterly in the dark. Yet you must act. You have no alternative but to choose—'it is not

[1] *Pensées*, 195.

optional, You are embarked.'—and your choice must be affected
by the truth which you cannot know. So you are forced to wager,
the stake being your whole life.[1]

Now if we bet on there being a God and an after-life and
lose, we lose nothing, because if there is neither God nor immortality there is nothing to gain by winning. On the other
hand, if we bet on the non-existence of God and immortality
we lose an eternity of bliss if we are wrong and may suffer
eternal damnation. Faith, therefore, is more reasonable than
disbelief.[2]

This argument is wholly unacceptable and unavailing. In the
first place, if our ignorance is as deep as Pascal avers we cannot
formulate the alternatives as sharply and as exclusively as he
does. There are other possibilities. There may be a god or no
god, or there may be an evil demon, as Descartes assumed, and
he might take perverse pleasure in torturing believers throughout
eternity and rewarding atheists with endless mischievous amuse-
ments. One can almost imagine that this was Nietzsche's secret
hope. Again, the Manichean doctrine might be true, that there
is constant internecine strife between the powers of good and
evil, and whichever way we wager the victory might go to
Lucifer. The atheist might even prefer that alternative. But
aside from any of these picturesque speculations, Pascal's argument is morally bankrupt.

If I am to wager on the existence of God and the truth of the
Christian religion, the presumption is that God is just and
benevolent and that his behest to man is love and selfless devotion. His grace supervenes upon duty that is done only for
Christ's sake and faith that is freely given. If my wager is
motivated by nothing but the weight of the odds on advantages
to be lost or gained—nothing other than fear of eternal damnation and a covetous desire for eternal bliss, I cannot but lose.
On the other hand, if, as we are taught, God is merciful and
forgiving, will he not exercise clemency to those who honestly
refuse to give credence where their intellect boggles; to those

[1] *Pensées*, 233.
[2] *Ibid.*

who sincerely reject inducements, of whatever kind, to betray their better judgment? This was Spinoza's course when the Amsterdam Synagogue offered him a stipend of Fl. 1000 to observe outwardly religious practices in which he no longer believed.

III

The foundation of faith can be neither ignorance nor craven cupidity, it must rest on something more solid and more honest. Nevertheless, Pascal is right that choose we must. We *are* embarked and have no option to suspend judgment. Judgment, however, cannot be confined to a calculation of chances for which no evidence is weighed. There must be some rational grounds. Pascal is also right to insist that the search for truth is of paramount importance to us and may be neglected only at our peril. We cannot bank on ultimate success, but, as we have no alternative but to seek, we likewise have no alternative but to believe in the reality of that rational ground which is the object of our search.

In yet another particular Pascal correctly points the way. Man is inescapably aware of his own insufficiency, his finiteness, his failings, his shortcomings and his wretchedness. And, at the same time, being thus aware, being impelled constantly to search for truth, having aspirations which admit no limit; being conscious of himself and his world, of his own littleness and the world's immeasurable greatness and complexity, man has a unique dignity and birthright that he refuses to surrender.[1] This contrast and apparent conflict affords the clue to what we seek, for to be aware of defect is at once to presuppose a criterion of perfection; to be cognizant of one extreme is *ipso facto* to be aware of both. Pascal sums up the matter thus: 'Know then proud man, what a paradox you are to yourself. Humble yourself, weak reason; be silent foolish nature; *learn that man infinitely transcends man,* and learn from your Master your true condition of which you are ignorant. Hear God.' (My italics).[2] That man infinitely transcends himself is the one

[1] Cf. *Pensées,* 397–424.
[2] *Pensées,* 434.

source of his self-enlightenment, and the final fruit of his reflection is self-abasement before the infinite refulgence of its ultimate object. But in saying this I am anticipating what should come later.

In spite of his criticism of Descartes, Pascal is at one with him on this point, for Descartes, having discovered the indubitability of his own awareness of himself and the undeniability of the existence of his consciousness, at once registers his acute awareness of his finiteness.

> 'Following upon this [the undeniable assurance of the existence of *Ego cogitans*], and reflecting on the fact that I doubted, and that consequently my existence was not quite perfect (for I saw clearly that it was a greater perfection to know than to doubt), I resolved to inquire whence I had learnt to think of anything more perfect than I myself was. . .' (*Discourse on Method,* Pt. IV, Haldane and Ross' translation).

And this leads him at once to the affirmation of the infinite, the acknowledgement of his possession of an idea of God.

To be aware of finitude whether in oneself or another, is *ipso facto* to be, at least implicitly, aware of a standard by which one judges finitude. In the very act of judging, the finite is transcended: both the judging and that which is judged are necessarily involved in this transcendence. For to be aware of my own deficiency I must be aware; and I must be aware of myself; I must be a self-conscious judging agent. And in making the judgment I must presuppose a criterion of judgment even if I am not explicitly aware of its complete and exact content.

Man is aware of himself. In his awareness of his abilities and his strengths, his knowledge and his achievements, such as they are, he is constantly and inevitably aware of his own weaknesses, and inabilities, his uncertainties and ignorance, his incapacities and shortcomings. He cannot fail, if he is aware of the former, to be aware of their limitations; and in these limitations he can never rest. His inadequacies are perpetually irksome to him. He finds fulfilment and satisfaction, if at all, only on the side of adequacy, and thus identifies himself, as fulfilled, with the standard of completion, by which he, at the same time, judges his own shortcomings. In knowing himself as inadequate he transcends his own finiteness.

'The greatness of man is great,' writes Pascal, 'in that he knows himself to be miserable. A tree does not know itself to be miserable. It is then being miserable to know oneself to be miserable; but it is also being great to know that one is miserable.'[1]

In short, the greatness of man is that he *knows* himself, and in knowing himself he knows his littleness, and in knowing his littleness he transcends his own diminutive stature. He transcends it in that he is aware of it, as such. It is this self-awareness that nullifies and defeats, that rejects and abrogates, all the efforts of atheism to restrict the world, man and his knowledge to the merely finite.

The being, *das Dasein,* of man's consciousness cannot be doubted or denied. But not only in its present evidence to his mind, but equally in its occurrence in the natural world and in his endeavours to explain both that world and his own place in it, consciousness compels him to go beyond the merely finite and to discover, even in that, evidences of an infinite self-warranting totality that is the object and affirmation of theism.

IV

Atheism, as we have seen, seeks to rest in science, in the material workings of nature and in man as a natural product. But what consistent account can be given of any of these as the atheist tries to conceive them? Science is the effort to become systematically aware of, that is, to understand, the workings of nature. But how is science to understand that understanding awareness itself? Science, to be science must entertain an idea of nature as a system of phenomena obeying natural laws. But these ideas of nature and of natural laws cannot themselves

[1] *Pensées,* 397.

be treated as phenomena within the system. Only a conscious subject can be aware of nature, as nature, and only a conscious subject can conceive of laws as general and universal. But to bring the conscious subject itself under the laws which it conceives is impossible, because to be aware of oneself as subject to law is *ipso facto* to transcend one's subjection to it in making the law an object of one's understanding. A law is a universal relationship of certain terms. To know it, the subject of the knowledge must comprehend in one and the same act of awareness all the terms so related. It cannot therefore be limited to or identified with any of the terms coming under the law, and so cannot be subject to it. As Kant showed, the original synthetic unity of apperception cannot be brought under the categories of which it is itself the source.

This difficulty was precisely what we encountered in our criticism of Freud, and it is inescapable in all psychology, which is the attempt to give a scientific account of consciousness. Either it must adopt a purely behaviorist standpoint, in which case consciousness, and inevitably that of the theorizing psychologist is excluded from the object of study. Or else it must objectify—phenomenalize—the working of the mind, and so forfeit its ability to account, by its discovered laws, for the conscious activity of the mind which is objectifying and giving the account of the phenomena. If the psychologist's own consciousness in his psychological theorizing were made subject to the laws he discovers, for example, if it were accountable as rationalization, or sublimation of repressed cathexes, or the product of instinctive urge, or whatever natural causal principle you choose, the theory itself (as we saw earlier) would automatically become invalid as a statement about the facts. This does not invalidate psychology as a science. It only sets limits to science as explanation of natural phenomena within which it may not and cannot include itself without invalidating its own theory as a statement of truth. To treat science as a social phenomenon subject to the laws (whatever they may be) of sociology, as has recently been done by some writers, immediately has the effect of subjectivising all scientific theory, making it relative purely to a special community and so depriving it of its validity as objective knowledge. Then either we must exempt from the conclusion the sociological theory itself, or else it becomes tainted by its own strictures and is rendered worthless. Consequently, science must transcend itself to remain science. It stands as evidence that something beyond its own limits is inherent in the very consciousness which makes it possible.

The same conclusion is forced upon us if we reflect upon the theories of nature which science itself offers us. Here we return to the sort of critique we offered earlier of Engel's dialectic of nature. We may dispose at the outset of materialism in the strict sense of the word: that is, the thesis that basically nothing exists in the universe except crass unorganized matter, to which all else can be reduced without remainder. In accordance with that thesis, consciousness would be understood in some sense to be a property of matter, as such. If the properties of matter are, however, limited to the mechanical, no account whatsoever of consciousness is possible, for the concepts of mass, force and momentum give no clue to its manifest nature. If it is sought somehow to reduce the mind to the brain and the brain to a machine, consciousness is simply left out of account altogether. Many things may be explicable by cybernetics which perhaps were inexplicable before, but consciousness is not one of them. It is quite inconceivable how any complex of servo-mechanisms could be aware of itself. Some scientists delude themselves into believing the contrary because while they assert that servo-mechanisms depend on feed-back and that what is fed back is 'information'; they define that term in a technical sense as negative entropy, and that obscures its proper meaning: namely knowledge consciously apprehended. Yet that meaning is surreptitiously imported into their argument, although it is not what their definition acknowledges. Every such mechanism has to be designed, constructed and programmed, and the 'information' it handles, in the technical sense of the word, has to be encoded and decoded by conscious scientists, who understand it in the proper sense, and whose function in doing all this cannot be replaced by servo-mechanisms. No machine can program itself; nor can any construct itself from unstructured matter—the second law of thermodynamics forbids it, and the 18th century despair of perpetual motion bears witness to it. If it be alleged that organisms are no more than machines capable of constructing and programming other machines like themselves, the line of descent must be traceable back either to infinity or to some unprogrammed programmer. In short, to maintain any such doctrine we must resuscitate, in a new and modernized form, the Cosmological Argument for the existence of God. The finite has once again forced us to transcend it.

To be plausible, therefore, materialism must be made dialectical, that is to say we must introduce into it some principle of evolution from gross matter to higher forms. Mere complication is not enough for this purpose, for no mere complication of gross matter, however intricate, brings us one step nearer to life and consciousness. Bigger and better molecules, however helical and involuted they may be, explain precisely nothing of teleological process and conscious awareness. That life involves teleology, even Jacques Monod, the arch-materialist in biochemistry, admits by implication when he postulates teleonomy as essential to organisms and defines it as the achievement of 'un projet,' or accomplishment of a design.[1]

But if we admit that mind develops out of matter, by whatever means, we have already abandoned strict materialism. For whatever evolves from an earlier form must in some manner be present potentially in the more primitive. If then mind is to emerge from matter there must be that in the nature of matter which is more than merely physical and which renders such development possible. The final outcome of evolution must somehow be present in the primordial substance and must be immanent throughout the process. Otherwise its eventual fruition is incomprehensible and would be sheerly miraculous, and in speaking of evolution we should be using a word without significant meaning.

Moreover contemporary scientific theory provides us with just such an immanent principle. Contemporary physics, as was

[1] Cf. *Le Hasard et la Necessité* (Paris, 1970), pp. 31–33.

mentioned earlier is no longer mechanistic, and (*pace* Marx and Engels) not even materialistic. Matter itself, in the form of elementary particles, is conceived as the manifestation of prior forms of structure, such as superposed waves—what Schroedinger called a *Gestalt* imposed upon some undetectable sub-flux of energy.[1] Pauli's Principle of Exclusion has the effect of imposing structure—or form—on all associations of particles; and what increases in complexity as we go up the scale from electrons to macro-molecules and beyond, is not 'gross matter' but organized systems. In short, primordial in nature is some principle of order which develops continuously into a scale of increasingly complex and more highly integrated forms.

To trace this gamut through all its phases is beyond the scope of these lectures.[2] What is significant is that consciousness, whatever else it may or may not be, is an activity of organizing and integrating the elements of sentient awareness, through the agency of attention, issuing in percipience and judgment. Some such activity of organization and integration is found to be present primordially in physical reality. So if we could find a dialectical principle which was capable of linking the two we should be able to understand how a conscious organism might by stages be generated from inorganic matter. But if we succeeded in doing this we should have demonstrated that nature itself contains the seed of its own self-transcendence, for once become conscious of itself an organism is, as we have seen, aware of its own limitations and has thus transcended them. If, besides, it is the expression of a universal tendency to self-completion, it will inevitably refuse to rest in the limitations it discovers and will persistently aspire after a perfection which lies beyond its merely finite aspect.

And that surely is implicit in the very nature of organization and structure. For a structure or organized pattern is a systematic whole, the principle of unity of which is not, and cannot be reduced to, the mere aggregate of its parts. They cannot

[1] Cf. *What is Life? and Other Essays*, (New York, 1956) p. 177.
[2] I have attempted it in outline in *The Foundations of Metaphysics in Science* (London, 1965).

determine it, but it determines their inter-relations and coherence, in fact the very nature and existence of the parts. Any finite entity, therefore, must, *qua* finite, be an incomplete or defective system. Its tendency must therefore be, in order to be truly and fully what it really is, towards completion of the system. That completion would, however, have to be total and all-embracing. It would thus be absolute—or what Hegel called the true infinite.

If, as I have suggested elsewhere,[1] feeling is a specially high degree of integration of intense physiological activity in a living organism, and consciousness is the activity of discrimination and organization of feelings, the continuation of the series of forms beyond human experience must lead to something which is at least superior to human personality—something supra-personal —and the final consummation could not be below the level of consciousness.

V

Finally, let us turn to human experience as we know it. Let us, in short, consider the implications of Humanism, taking man as we find him and treating him as the crown of natural development. What, we must ask, is man? And no answer is tolerable which neglects his self-reflective capacity, his consciousness of himself and his surroundings, his overwhelming endeavour to know and understand his own nature and his place in and relationship to the world in which he finds himself. In action he seeks an ultimate satisfaction that he envisages as happiness; but this he cannot find in ephemeral pleasure, which at best he treats as a distraction. Satisfaction of natural desires does not content him, if only because they can hardly all be fulfilled harmoniously, and because their progressive fulfilment generates new needs which may not only conflict among themselves, but even with those from which they originated. Accordingly, his happiness requires the organization of his primary gratifications,

[1] *Vide Foundations of Metaphysics in Science,* Chs. XVI and XVII; and cf. Susanne Langer, *Mind, An Essay on Human Feeling* (Baltimore, 1967), Vol. I, Ch. II.

subordinating some to others, foregoing what conflicts with preferable attainments, and regulating conduct according to imperatives which give precedence to ends more highly valued. His satisfaction must be a total fulfilment of the self which he sees as a justification of his existence and he will be content with nothing less.

Such total fulfilment in practice is not separable from the first demand for understanding man's place in the scheme of things; partly because it depends on the adequacy of our self-knowledge which is inseparable from our relation to the rest of the world.[1] And knowledge of this is necessary to self-fulfilment also, because we see no sense in an existence which seems totally self-involuted. The mere spectacle of continual generation, sustenance and death of individuals appears to us as futile unless it ministers to something more significant, and if it does so this can be seen only in some aspect of our relation to others and the world at large. If man feels himself isolated and alone pursuing a futile existence in a vast universe of dead, unheeding matter (the kind of world to which he is abandoned by atheism), he is oppressed by a sense of utter forlornness and gives way to despair. Such is the sense of sheer absurdity and meaninglessness of things to which some Existentialist philosophers point. But neither is despair a final refuge, and those who see things in this way find solace in the acclamation of their own freedom, evidenced in every choice, even of suicide.

Once again, the finite is here transcended, for freedom, if we enjoy it, is the fruit of our consciousness of self as rising above the mere accidental circumstances in which we find ourselves, and subordinating them and our own predicament to the exercise of our own untrammelled will. But that is not the whole of the matter. Freedom is no mere arbitrary caprice, and choice is always between alternatives requiring evaluation and implying

[1] To quote Pascal once more: 'Man, for instance, is related to all he knows. He needs a place wherein to abide, time through which to live, motion in order to live, elements to compose him, warmth and food to nourish him, air to breathe. He sees light; he feels bodies; in short, he is in a dependent alliance with everything. To know man, then it is necessary to know. . . the whole. . .' (*Pensées*, 72.).

preference. And that again involves judgment. As Hegel puts it, 'He who speaks of freedom and neglects thought does not know what he is saying.' Freedom cannot be sheer indeterminacy for that is unaccountable and would render the will uncontrollable, even by the agent claiming to be free. Free action can only be determinate conduct, but its liberty consists in its not being subject to external coercion. It is, as the great philosophers have mostly realized, *self*-determination. And that is precisely the essential character of thought and the human action expressive of it.

Thought, however, is that principle of organizing and integrating, distinguishing and unifying differences, which is active in all consciousness, and, as Kant well saw, alone makes the experience of objects possible. Likewise, as Kant well saw, the demands of thought (that is, of the intellect) do not stop short of the conception of an all embracing whole of reality, complete and self-sufficient, an Ideal of Reason, without which, as he says, we should have no adequate criterion of empirical truth whatever.[1] In short, the finite transcends itself again in this manner; Kant's declaration, that human reason is compelled to raise questions which it cannot answer is simply another pointer to this fact. Moreover, despite the limitations he sets to the understanding, Kant does answer the questions he declares, to be insoluble by human reason, even though not all subsequent philosophers have accepted his answers. For our purpose here, however, the main significance of Kant's teaching is that human reason is inevitably transcendent beyond finite experience, and however admonished by Kant, cannot rest in the finite.

Some further investigation of Kant's treatment of this issue will throw light upon our topic. Our conception of the ideas of reason, freedom, immortality and God, Kant sees as the inevitable consequence of the nature of our minds and the experience of which they are capable. But these ideas, he tells us, because they go beyond sensuous experience, do not apply to phenomena. Nor do they apply to things in themselves, because things in themselves are inaccessible to our knowledge.

[1] *Critique of Pure Reason*, A657, B679.

The objects of the ideas of reason are only noumena, only constructs of the mind. Whether or not there are realities corresponding to them (with one exception to which I shall presently return) is problematical and may not be categorically asserted. The use of these ideas of reason cannot, therefore, be constitutive of objects but only regulative and heuristic.

In the *Critique of Pure Reason,* the argument of the Dialectic seeks to demonstrate the invalidity of the traditional proofs of God's existence. Kant was neither the first nor the last philosopher to deny their cogency, but he has been unquestionably the most influential. It might seem at first sight, that, in doing so, Kant gives support to atheism, for the atheist could maintain that we can know nothing besides natural phenomena, that the ideas of reason, whether or not we are inescapably liable to entertain them, are, as Kant says, illusions, and we have no good grounds for any belief in God. But Kant himself did not adopt this position. He held ideas of reason to be illusory only so far as they claimed objective status. Things in themselves, even if unknowable, he held to be real. That God existed was always a possibility which, though we could not prove it, for him remained open. Thus he claimed to have secured for faith what was inaccessible to science. In fact, in the later Critiques he found good grounds for asserting more positively that there is a God and that the thing-in-itself must be of the nature of mind.

There is, in particular, one link between noumena and reality which Kant finds secure and which enables him to offer a proof of God's reality which he considers sound, and this once more is clear evidence of the transcendence of the finite. The whole possibility of any experience whatsoever depends on the categories, and the categories themselves are but the principles of order derivative from the unity of the transcendental subject of consciousness, the I = I, whose indubitable existence Descartes established. The transcendental ego cannot be a phenomenal object, it cannot be made subject to its own categories, and the empirical self, which we can observe, is only an appearance of it. But, by the same token, the activity of the noumenal subject is not conditioned by the laws of nature, and as moral agent it conducts itself as a free, self-determined will. Of this free agency we are intuitively aware in our practical life, and although we can experience the effects of our actions only as phenomena in the natural world, which are determined by natural laws (psychological and other), our own existence as noumenal agents is assured. It proclaims itself in the unconditional decree of its own moral law which makes duty a categorical imperative. This is the law which reason itself imposes the sole aim of which is to realize in phenomenal experience its own ideal.

Obedience to the moral law is man's duty. It is for him an imperative because his sensuous nature requires and offers other incentives to action than respect for the law of reason, but that is the only incentive which duty permits. The effort of man to perfect his nature, which is his duty, is thus a perpetual struggle between two principles, one good and one evil. Human nature being what it is, indefinite time is needed for ultimate success. But because it is man's duty to purify his will, it must be possible, as 'ought' implies 'can.' It is also man's duty (and therefore possible) to bring about the greatest good achievable, and that would include universal happiness. Again happiness, though it may not be a motive for doing one's duty, should in all justice be its result. But neither does our experience give evidence that man can perfect his own nature solely by his own effort, nor that happiness is the result even of the most well intentioned morally right action. However, as these consequences must be possible if it is our duty to bring them about, we must postulate the existence of an all-powerful benevolent ruler of the world, who ensures that ultimately they will be realized. By his Grace he supplements men's moral efforts and by his Providence he makes the morally good happy in the last reckoning. A similar reasoning establishes for Kant the immortality of the soul.

This moral argument for God's existence is not successful, for even though man's reason did impose a moral law upon him to realize its ideal, if that ideal is merely subjective and noumenal, as Kant alleges, no necessity ensues of invoking a divine power to make the experienced world conform to it, where man by his own effort fails. Morality and the categorical imperative on this basis might be as problematic as religion. Kant makes it depend in the final issue upon an inescapable, though inscrutable, intuition of its certainty. No more proof of God's existence is thereby provided than by any of the traditional arguments, which Kant rejects for epistemological reasons.

But the importance of Kant's theory is its insistence upon the inevitable self-transcendence of human reason. It conceives an ideal indispensable to its knowledge of the phenomenal world, the actualization of which in practice it imposes inexorably upon itself as a duty. And this generates an aspiration beyond its empirical life to a reality which is wholly perfect and complete.

The ontological status of this ideal remains in question because Kant at the outset has denied objective status to ideas of reason. In the case of the *Ens realissimum,* the idea of God, his rejection of its objective status depends on his refutation of the Ontological Argument—that its essence involves existence. But here Kant's reasoning is itself at fault. He argues that existence is not a predicate, that *no* idea, even of a being completely perfect, can therefore contain it. The idea of a hundred imaginary dollars contains the same predicates as do a hundred real dollars. The difference is only empirical evidence. Existence, in effect, implies empirically presented relationships and without them nothing follows from a mere idea as to its object's reality. But Kant himself has shown that empirical evidence is possible only under categories whose source is the transcendental subject, and that reason itself and its ideal is indispensable to any criterion of empirical truth. His refutation, in effect, asserts that only what can be brought under the categories can be said to exist, and that the Ideal cannot be brought under the categories. But the Ideal is, on his own showing, the condition under which alone the categories can ever be applied. Hence the very premises of Kant's argument against the Ontological

Proof presuppose the ideal of reason, the *Ens realissimum,* the reality of which it repudiates.

Of course, regarding existence as a merely phenomenal manifestation it would be, as Hegel pointed out, inept to try to prove that God exists. Of course the Ideal of Reason cannot be brought under the categories. Only what is finite is subject to natural law. It is therefore ridiculous to predicate phenomenal existence of God. But the superior reality of that which is the ground and condition of all phenomenal existence certainly cannot be denied if anything is to be said to exist at all. Accordingly, the transcendence of the finite to which Kant's philosophy testifies, leads unfailingly to theism.

Kant's rejection of the Ontological Argument is thus out of harmony with the whole thrust and trend of his philosophy, which does, in fact, supply the basis on which Hegel later reinterpreted and reinstated the traditional proof of God's existence. From Kant's own reasoning it becomes apparent that the same necessity which compels us to assert the existence of our own consciousness in *Cogito ergo sum,* compels us likewise to affirm the existence, as the condition of all empirical knowledge, of one unified system of variegated reality—the condition and presupposition of all science. For it is only as related to the one transcendental subject that the objects of experience can be apprehended and related to one another. All such relations are therefore synthesized into a single system, the objective content of one experience grasped in the original unity of transcendental apperception.

The idea of this unified totality of the world is at the same time the Ideal of Reason which Kant identifies as God. Frequently objection is raised to this identification: The unified whole of nature, it is said, is not God except for the Pantheist; and this objection, so far as it goes, is sound; for Kant's ideal does seem to be the unity of nature as constructed and synthesized by the understanding. It is the ideal of empirical science. We have already found, however, that that ideal is not and cannot be self-sufficient but points beyond itself through its very failure to include in its scope the understanding which comprehends it. Only when it is recognized as a dialectical structure embodying and expressing in its processes a principle of wholeness and integration, which continuously develops through its forms, until it manifests itself to itself in human consciousness—only then do we begin to discern some premonition of its bourne.

A dialectical system is one in which a totality, immanent and potential in its least and most fragmentary constituent, is persistently driven by its own inner urge to self-fulfilment and self-completion. Nothing less or other than this can be the Ideal of Reason, and such a totality both includes, as one of its phases, and transcends in the drive to its self-fulfilment, the human consciousness, which (in its reflective stage), misapprehends it as a mechanical whole. It is not the totality of nature merely, but the totality immanent in nature, manifesting itself as nature, and coming to fruition through natural processes *as mind,* which attains self-awareness in man's consciousness, and through that again transcends itself to an absolute spiritual self-realization which is infinite in its self-sufficiency.

Such a whole and nothing less is what is to be identified with God—a God immeasurably beyond any pantheist divinity. It is such a whole that Hegel called Absolute Spirit and its reality is undeniable because, as we glimpsed earlier,[1] it is that which, as the ultimate system, is immanent in all the phases of development in nature up to man, and expresses itself in his conscious self-awareness, an undeniably existent awareness, at once of finiteness and insufficiency, and also, by implication, of infinitude. The existence of consciousness depends and proceeds from this infinity and so becomes the immediate evidence of its reality and necessity. Thus man in his own self-knowledge inevitably transcends himself, cannot rest in his own finiteness, but strains toward the infinite through an insurmountable urge and aspiration which expresses itself in his moral striving and his religious devotion.

[1] Cf. above, pp. 55-59.

VI

To be aware of my own finitude, I must be aware of an other, or a beyond, which limits me. If that other is also finite, in knowing my relation to him or it, I include both in one system and transcend the limits of both in so doing. If that system is still finite the same process repeats itself *ad infinitum,* or until an all inclusive whole is envisaged. But throughout this process it is the whole which is presupposed and which makes the process possible. Accordingly I could not be aware of myself as finite unless I were aware of an infinite, and I could not be aware of that unless it were immanent already in my thought. It is through immanence in consciousness of the absolute reality that consciousness is self-transcendent.

Thus if God did not exist I could have no idea of him, and so none of my own finite being. But of this latter I am invincibly certain. Hence theism is inescapable. As consciousness is self-transcendent and the conscious subject cannot consistently deny its own existence, if it denies the existence of God, it must identify itself as deity. Thus Nietzsche declaims, 'Better no god, better to produce destiny on one's own account,; . . . better to be God oneself?'[1] But this very declaration is an expression of self-transcendence, for who more assiduously than Nietzsche complains of the finitude of man: yet he must at the very least, be a bridge to Superman.

Because atheism limits reality to phenomenal nature, knowledge to empirical science and man to his own human capacities, not even the atheist can rest in atheism. For finite nature transcends itself in man, science transcends itself in philosophy, and humanism transcends itself through man's self-reflective consciousness; and all together point beyond to an infinite reality which supplies the deficiencies each them suffers. The infinite reality is God. Man's self-transcendent awareness is the image of God immanent in his thinking; and the practical expression of the self-transcendence is his religious faith and his worship of the divine.

[1] *Also Sprach Zarathustra,* IV, 'Retired from Service'.

Chapter IV

THE RATIONAL BASIS OF THEISM

I

Throughout the foregoing discussion the assumption has been allowed that, if theism is to be accepted at all, it can be only upon faith, whether or not that faith may have some rational support. The first aim of the argument was to invalidate the claim of atheism to established knowledge. That we have accomplished and have been able besides to show that the arguments offered by atheists in support of their unbelief are hollow and self-defeating, that in fact they tend towards the opposite conclusion and require us in each case to affirm an inescapable self-transcendence of the finite. But the assumption that theism is purely a product of faith is dogmatic and arbitrary unless similar reasoning can dispose of all claim to conclusive rational demonstration, and no such reasoning has, as yet, been examined. We must inquire what rational arguments can be produced and whether they can be sustained.

The arguments that have, in the past, been offered for the existence of God have been attacked and criticized variously throughout the centuries, and have nevertheless been revived and restated in new forms, only to be attacked afresh by new refutations. But before we consider the traditional proofs in their many diverse forms, or the arguments that have been opposed to them from time to time and are offered afresh today, we must say something about the nature of rational thinking in general; for, contrary to common opinion, not all rationality is of the same kind. Logic is not an invariant system of fixed and static rules governing thought at any and every level. Even formal logic has not remained unchanged since it was first systematized by Aristotle, and formal logic itself is appropriate only to a certain level of thinking. There is another logic which is universal in its scope, but, as I shall try briefly to show in what follows, it is not uniform in its operation at every stage of intellectual development. This is because intellect is not a static faculty but a constantly growing and developing function of the mind, the principles of whose activity evolve with the insight that it achieves. The universal logic, therefore, displays itself in specifically different forms in different phases of thinking, of which formal logic (in any of its forms) is only one. Accordingly, we shall find that there are different kinds of rationalism and that what is accounted 'reasonable' at one level may reveal itself as altogether stultifying at another, not because it is sheerly irrational, but because, through oversight of wider issues, it defeats its own admitted end.

Speaking broadly, rational arguments may be either of two different kinds, for reason itself functions on at least two different levels. There is the rationality of what Hegel called the understanding, and also the speculative reason which rejects the mere analysis of the understanding while it transmutes it at a higher level into a philosophical rationality that 'understands' both analytically and synthetically at the same time. Such reasoning is analysis and synthesis in one, functioning as two moments of thought which, though they must be distinguished, cannot be separated, and which coalesce in a more enlightened comprehension than either by itself can achieve. Speculative reason, because it is both analytic and synthetic at once, is dialectical; and dialectic is the self-analysing activity of a synthetic unity, which thereby generates itself out of rudiments that constitute its own elements.

To the understanding this sounds nonsensical, for it is surely palpable that nothing can generate the rudiments out of which it develops itself. Until such rudiments are present that which emerges from them is not there to generate anything, let alone the source from which it must itself originate. However the contradiction is due to the inadequacy of the descriptive terms at our disposal. Dialectic is not merely a linear process of development from a point source or epigenetic germ, although any such linear process involves and manifests a dialectical principle; but the essential dialectic itself is a self-explication of a whole which is immanent throughout the entire process, in every moment and phase, and at every stage. Any beginning or rudiment is therefore only apparent. It already contains the whole implicitly and may, from a different point of view, appear equally as a product or result. Likewise, the totality, as a developed outcome of the process, reveals itself equally as the beginning and source of everything that was involved in the process of its own development. That process can occur only if the totality is already in some sense actual, and the whole can be actualized only in and through the process. Thus we speak of a whole which is at once eternally realized and continually realizing itself by means of a process throughout which it is immanent. Such immanent wholeness as the source of inner dynamic is incomprehensible to the understanding, which can conceive totality only as aggregation and universality only in terms of class inclusion, or subsumption, or con-notation (where the prefix 'con' signifies collection); but a dialectical system has quite other implications, the nature of which I shall presently attempt to outline further.

It must immediately be apparent from what has been said that dialectic is at once a logical and a metaphysical concept. The logical relations it defines and determines are those consequent upon a metaphysical structure, which, being dynamic in character, is also a process. It is a process, therefore, both logical and actual, so that Hegel wrote truly of dialectic when he said that 'it is the principle of all movement, all life and all activity in the actual world.'[1]

The antithesis of the two levels of reasoning above-mentioned is well illustrated by the historical adventures of the traditional proofs of God's existence. Fundamentally these proofs are expressions of metaphysical reasoning grounded in a dialectic, which they do not always adequately disclose. But they have repeatedly been stated in forms appropriate to the logic of the understanding and so, by that same logic, have been criticised as invalid, only to be reasserted as the utterance of a persistent metaphysical insight seeking its dialectical demonstration. The

[1] *Encyclopädie* §87, *Zus.* 1.

oscillation between proof and refutation is continuous from Anselm and Guanilo, to Descartes and Caterus, from Leibniz and Kant to Hegel and Kierkegaard. In our own day Colling-wood declared that, since Hegel's re-establishment of the Onto-logical Argument, it had not been seriously challenged, only to incite Gilbert Ryle to protest against the disregard of what he hailed as 'one of the biggest advances in logic that has been made since Aristotle, namely . . . the discovery that particular matters of fact cannot be the implicates of general propositions'.[1] Since then the argument has been reaffirmed by Charles Hart-shorne and by Norman Malcolm and re-refuted by a whole covey of analytical critics. No good purpose will be served by reviewing the detailed course of this debate, but some indication may be given in principle of how and why it has occurred.

The formal logic of the understanding is based on the uni-versal abstractly conceived. Such language nowaday sounds obsolete and outdated, for few, if any, modern logicians speak of universals. But they are not averse to speaking of classes and of sets, an important part of their logic being a calculus of classes, and set theory a still more advanced development. It is as a collection of particulars that contemporary logicians conceive a class, the members of which are identified by certain specifiable resemblances. A resemblance, or set of resemblances, is thus the presupposed criterion of membership in a class—a common property or a group of such properties. But this is precisely the conception of the abstract universal: a quality or property common to and abstracted from a number of particulars and serving as the hall-mark for their membership of an assignable class. This is the latent foundation of the contemporary theory of quantification, according to which particulars are collected together in classes as their resembling qualities or properties occur regularly together.

$$(x) \ (\Phi x \ \supset \ \Psi x)$$

'For all x, if x is Φ, then x is Ψ', defines the class of x's which are both Φ and Ψ. But $\Phi x \ \supset \ \Psi x$ is purely hypothetical as is

[1] G. Ryle, 'Mr. Collingwood and the Ontological Argument', *Mind*, XLIV, No. 174, 1935, p. 142.

shown by its form, and the constant conjunction of Φ and Ψ must be discovered empirically. Though it may be proposed hypothetically, its actual occurrence in reality requires instantiation, which can never be deduced from the mere hypothesis.

$(\exists a)(\Phi a)$: 'there is an a such that a is Φ' does not follow from the class-concept above defined and can be asserted only on the strength of empirical evidence. Accordingly, by this logic, existence can never be inferred from general terms alone or from their conjunction. Its establishment always requires empirical premisses. It cannot be deduced *a priori*.

It follows likewise that existence cannot be necessary but is always contingent, for what is necessarily, or universally true, can only be a conjunction of properties which is always hypothetical: $(x)(\Phi x \supset \Psi x)$, If anything is Φ it is Ψ, but that anything is Φ can only be subject to empirical discovery. The universal, being abstract, cannot specify itself; its specification depends on contingent experience. The only necessary truths are those which follow from the definition of terms. They are all analytic and tautological.[1]

This is the logic of the understanding, according to which rationality consists in conformity to analytical formal deduction and to inductive generalization from empirical evidence. No other form of reasoning is permitted or recognized and doctrines which cannot be supported by either of these two forms of reasoning are castigated as either false or meaningless, unscientific and mystical.

---

[1] Contemporary logicians commonly deny that formal logic presupposes (tacitly or otherwise) any form of metaphysic—and my contention above implies that it does. In fact, I am convinced that an underlying metaphysic can always be revealed by careful examination of its doctrines, its rules and the way they are manipulated. An uninterpreted calculus can be applied only if its transformation rules are regarded as rules of inference and they can only be taken as such if they or some other feature of the calculus is assumed to correspond in some way to the nature of the things to which the calculus is being applied. Upon what the nature of things is taken to be will depend whether or not the calculus can be interpreted. And to decide that it cannot be interpreted is to affirm in effect that there is nothing in reality with reference to which its rules can function as laws of inference. In what sense an uninterpretable calculus is logic at all may well be questioned, for of what could it be the logic?

Traditionally proofs of God's existence have been cast in forms which, though they have not always been those of modern symbolic logic, have nevertheless been dictated by the logic of the understanding and have accordingly been subject to refutation on its principles. They have sought to prove, by using arguments presentable in such formulae as those illustrated above, that a necessarily existing being is implied in the definition of God, or in any contingent existence, or in orderly arrangement empirically evident in nature. Every such proof involves the allegedly fallacious assumption that existence can be necessary and the fallacious process from the hypothetical to the categorical. But these are fallacious only according to the logic of the understanding and on the basis of epistemological and metaphysical assumptions which have been called in question by a whole range of thinkers from Hegel to F. H. Bradley and Brand Blanshard, as well as Karl, Popper, Thomas Kuhn and Imri Lakatos. They are assumptions which have not been and cannot be sustained, and others must be sought as the groundwork of our logical procedures.

II

If the world is to any extent intelligible its elements must constitute and must be comprehensible in some form of inter-related system constituting a single whole. If it is ultimately unintelligible, science and philosophy must in the final issue collapse and no knowledge would have sustainable grounds. In that case, the principle of sufficient reason could never be satisfied and scepticism total and complete must be the only possible outcome of inquiry. Scepticism (other than a provisional methodological device for eliminating error) is theoretically a self-contradictory and impossible position, involving theoretical incoherence which invades and paralyses action in the practical sphere; accordingly, the inescapable and fundamental presupposition of all knowledge, and *ipso facto* of all intelligent action, is the existence of a world at least in some degree intelligible.

But intelligibility in any degree implies a series or scale of degrees measurable in terms of a standard or absolute intelligibility, and this scale as a whole, from any assumed gradation up to the absolute which gives any grade its value and meaning, constitutes a single system. A world, or any other subject, which is in some degree intelligible, must thus belong to, and must at least partially reveal, a completely intelligible system which is wholly and exclusively self-sufficient. It is not just that the partially intelligible logically implies the fully intelligible, but that intelligibility of any degree involves systematic structure of some sort, and systematic structure is, by its very nature, characteristic of some totality. It cannot exist or be recognized in a form which is irremediably partial. Irremediable fragmentariness is in effect the denial of all system, which is the reason why there can be no apparent order which rests ultimately upon total chaos, and why ultimate unintelligibility in any partial respect invades and destroys all knowledge. Partial system must either be in principle capable of completion or else it is illusory and is not even partially systematic. The arc of a circle must be the arc of a complete circle to be an arc at all, and the same is true of any part of any conceivable pattern.

A systematic structure is not a class. It is neither a mere collection of particulars nor a common property of any such aggregation. Its elements may have in common nothing except their conformity to the principle of organization that determines the structure of the whole. And that principle is, above all, a principle of wholeness determining and requiring self-completion. It governs and regulates the entire content of the system, including the nature and mutual relationships of the parts, and so is universal to them all; but it is actualized, expressed and manifested only in those parts and their mutual inter-relations. It is specified in them and as their mutual disposition, in determining which it generates and specifies itself.

The organizing principle of such a system is thus the universal, or generic essence, of its specific manifestations—that is, of its elements or 'parts'. The word 'parts' is used here with reservations, and so is written between inverted commas, because it must not be misread as meaning bits or pieces the aggregation of which compiles the whole. They are parts in

the sense of constituents, but they constitute not by juxta-
position simply, but by mutual adaptation and complementation
of interlocking and contraposed differences. The inter-relation-
ship is of the kind felicitously and appropriately called in Fichte's
terminology, *Wechselwirkung* or *Wechselbestimmung;* and that
between part and whole is the relation between a particular expression or manifestation of a principle of structure and the
complete realization of that principle in the total design. The
principle is thus universal to its particular manifestations and
is immanent in them as an algebraical function is expressed by
and immanent in a spatial figure—in all its parts and their
mutual disposition—in analytic geometry.

A principle of this kind is rightly called a concrete universal,
and the product of its self-specification is what elsewhere I have
termed a polyphasic unity. The logic of its structure and explication must be wholly different from any based upon the abstract
concept of a class or aggregate (though that in certain contexts
may be presentable as a phase or feature of its development).
Its appropriate logic will be dialectical in character, as system
itself is dialectical in form—a form that is inseparable from and
properly identical with content. It is so because the whole is
immanent in each part and informs each part with the generic
or structural principle of the whole, so that in consequence each
part itself assumes a holistic character, and the totality is (as
Leibniz and Whitehead divined) an organic whole of organic
wholes. How this comes about we shall presently see; meanwhile we must take care not to imagine that the constituent
microcosms are coordinate in status. It would be wrong even to
picture them as occupying consecutive levels of coordinate
grouping. These may well be arrangements serving certain
limited or special purposes, but any such conception properly
examined will resolve itself into a serial and hierarchical order
in the manner next to be explained.

III

Every manifold is a multiplicity of elements in relation, and every relation is a link between overlapping terms. This controversial assertion can most expeditiously be defended by considering examples which appear *prima facie* to be most obviously contrary to it. (i) The relation between two separated points in space is no other than the distance between them (if only two are considered, direction has no distinct meaning). But the distance between two points is the length of the geodesic which joins them. This is a line consisting of points no two of which can be considered as adjacent—that is, as excluding an intermediary. The infinite divisibility of space guarantees the continuity of the flux of any such line. The relation between any two points on it, therefore, is a function of the flow, or overlap of all the consecutive points which make up the line. This may be only another way of stating the fact about space which supports the definition of a point given by Whitehead in terms of 'abstractive sets', that is, a set of regions of which any two members are such that one of them includes the other nontangentially and no region is included in every member of the set. A point is then a geometrical element to which such a set converges.[1] Any two points on a line must involve the overlap of the abstractive sets which define them. (ii) The relation between two colours depends on their respective positions in the continuous gradation of the spectrum where the overlap of hues is manifest and undeniable. (iii) the relation between two numbers is a function of the number continuum where consecutive digits are never so disparate as to preclude the intermediation of infinite avatars of fractional series.

The separation of terms in any of these examples is possible only by the intervention of continuously overlapping intermediaries, which overlap with each of the originals, so that it is only by means of the continuum that relations can be established. Examples could be multiplied, but without further profit, for it is clear that there can be no exceptions to the rule that a

[1] Cf. *Process and Reality* (Cambridge, 1929), pp. 421–423.

continuum of some sort is the matrix of any conceivable relation between any distinguishable terms.

A continuum, to be continuous involves heterogeneity of parts, for unless the parts are distinguishable they cannot continuously diverge. On the other hand, they equally cannot be totally heterogeneous and must be uniform and alike in some respects if they are to be continuous. It is this element of homogeneity that accounts for their overlap. Nevertheless, heterogeneity is indispensably necessary to continuity and a purely homogeneous continuum is as impossible as a square circle. Accordingly, every continuum will constitute some kind of a scale or progression of successively diverging forms.

Continuity thus involves both identity and difference and what varies continuously is that same property which is universal to the whole. For example, the spectrum of colour is a continuous divergence of hue from red to orange, to yellow, to green, to blue, to violet, and what changes is just the common property—hue, or, if you prefer it, wave-length. The universal, therefore, is at one and the same time what varies progressively and what remains constant, and this without any contradiction or conflict. Contradiction—or contrast—occurs only between the variants, so far as, despite overlap, they are mutually incompatible (e.g. the different colours, red, green, yellow, blue, etc.), and these are the specific differences, the species of the genus which is universal. And the unity is self-specified: colour without hue is not colour; to be colour at all it must specify itself into colour of continuously varying hue. Magnitude without measure is not magnitude, and to be magnitude it must specify itself as a scale of numbers. Hence the universal essence, to be at all, must involve the gamut of its specific forms, without which it is nothing, and the specific forms in their series must be embodiments of the generic essence, without which their specific character is lost.

This is the fundamental character and structure of all system, although it may be complicated in numerous ways which more or less obscure the general pattern. It is the fundamental structure because all system is a complex of relations between different elements unified by a universal principle of order, and, as we have seen, all relation is between overlapping terms in a continuum of heterogeneous constituents unified by an identical pervasive character.

Thus every system is a scale of forms in which the generic or universal essence is at once all-pervasive, and progressively varying.[1] As universal it is all-pervasive, and as progressively varying it specifies itself into particular instances. As it is the generic essence which is equally the variant element, the universal is immanent in each and every specific variation—light (or colour) is the immanent principle of every hue, magnitude of every number. But what is more difficult to see and to demonstrate, but none the less true, is that as the scale of specification progresses each successive species (or instance) is a more adequate expression than its predecessor of the universal essence. In the colour series this is not immediately apparent (although, if regarded as a succession of ascending frequencies of electromagnetic radiation, it becomes more so); in the number series it is slightly more evident, for the larger numbers are more obviously magnitudes than is zero or even one. But in more concrete cases it is undeniable that the more elaborate instances are, more properly than the less, what the generic essence truly is. Advantage is more truly good than pleasure, dutifulness better than advantage, and loving concern more genuinely good than duty. Yet all are specific cases of goodness, which is the generic essence of them all. And the reason why this progressive increase in adequacy is less apparent in the more abstract series than in the more concrete is precisely that the gamut of such series describes the structure of the world as a whole, revealing it as a scale of forms in which the true character of the scale (and thus of the world) is progressively more adequately manifested as we ascend its steps. The higher rungs (the more concrete series) display its character more fully and are explanatory of the lower, which they presuppose and incorporate. This is what was meant earlier by saying that the

[1] Cf. R. G. Collingwood, *An Essay on Philosophical Method*, Ch. III; and my *Foundations of Metaphysics in Science*, Ch. XXII.

totality was hierarchical and was an organic whole constituted of organic wholes. For the essential nature of wholeness is that the parts are explicable, as they are determined and generated, by the principle of wholeness which is immanent in each and every one of them, while it is fully actualized in their complete totality.

A corollary of this reasoning is that the scale of forms constituting the system cannot go on indefinitely. The specific variations cannot proliferate *ad infinitum* (in the spurious sense of infinity). We have known since Hegel that endless finitude is not the true infinite, and a series of forms progressively expressing a principle of wholeness more adequately advances towards a completeness and totality which is absolute, self-contained and self-sufficient. It is truly infinite.

A concrete universal or polyphasic unity is always hierarchical in structure and constitutes in consequence a developing series in which the whole is actualized only in, and as, the entire scale, while at the same time, this actualization is accomplished most fully only, in the final form. Paradoxical as it may seem at first, this final form is, therefore, not merely an end-state— no merely final form—but is the sublation, the preservation in itself and comprehension, of all the preceding forms. The ultimate realization of the whole and the complete self-specification of the universal which has been immanent throughout the process is at once the final form and the whole series. End and process coalesce and are, in the final issue, identical. The end is in the beginning, and the beginning is sublated in the end.

The process of self-specification of a universal principle in and as a scale of specific and progressively more adequate expressions of itself, by which, as a whole, it constitutes itself, is the dialectical process. And this dialectic is the higher rationality which renders its subject-matter intelligible in terms of generic essence and specific instantiation, through analytic synthesis (the differentiation of a unity) and synthetic analysis (the sublation and systematic comprehension of diverse specifications). It is rational by virtue of systematization, and not by virtue of mere dissection and aggregation.

The intelligible world is intelligible only as such a system and the 'proof' of the existence of any element in it, or of any character of it, is nothing other than the dialectical deduction of that element, or character, as a specific manifestation of the universal principle of the whole.

IV

Before we proceed further we must face the oft-repeated objection, that all this might well be a description of the way our minds work, but that it does not follow that the world answers to it. An *intelligible* world may be what we have maintained, but the real world may not be intelligible, and what we take to be real might be a mere projection of our subjective construction dictated by the nature and inherent working of our minds.

What this objection overlooks is that our minds and their subjective constructions are elements within the real world and must be accounted for in its terms. If they were not, if our imaginings and theoretical contrivings had no roots in, and no relation to, the world, which is their ostensible object, knowledge would be a meaningless word. If our subjective envisagements were *merely* and *purely* subjective we could not say of them that they represented a world at all, whether faithfully or discrepantly. A dichotomy between mind and the object of its knowledge makes knowledge impossible, for that is essentially a relation between subject and object, and a relation, as we have seen must be between overlapping parts of one continuum. Mind unrelated to the world can know nothing of the world and so cannot even suppose a world out of relation to itself. This is the underlying truth of Berkeley's epistemology.

But if there is a relation between the mind and the world which it knows, they must both belong to one system. The mind is, as nobody seriously doubts, a part and a product of nature and is integral to the world which it comes to know. Its knowledge must therefore be a manifestation of the principle of structure which determines the general character of the world. Or, to express the same thing otherwise, whatever principle of generation produces the variety of things in nature must also produce human beings and their thinking minds. There must be some generative principle in nature capable of producing our minds if they are ever to emerge. Consequently, we cannot assume a break between the actual world and ourselves and we must recognize an inevitable continuity between the world and our minds.

The dialectical conception of the world provides this continuity and makes it intelligible. If the world has dialectical structure, as I have demonstrated elsewhere[1] that it has, and if (as they are) our minds and our awareness of the world are a late phase in the dialectical scale, consciousness must be a developed form of the universal principle immanent in all natural beings and in every phase of natural process. It will, by the same token be a more adequate manifestation of that universal principle and it will sum up in itself, sublated and comprehended within it, all the prior phases—in short, it will develop, within itself and by its own proper activity, a knowledge of the world to which it belongs, by which it has been produced and from which it has been evolved, representing in the medium of consciousness all the phases prior and contributory to its own generation.

V

If, however, the world is a dialectical system, still more significant consequences follow. It follows upon what has just been said that the development in thought of the structure of the world—what we call science—will be a more adequate and complete manifestation of the principle of structure universal to reality as a whole than is any pre-scientific form. Science will be not only true of the world of nature, but, as Hegel expressed it, 'the truth of' that world. The rational awareness of the nature of the world transpires as what the world essentially is.[2] But

[1] Cf. *The Foundations of Metaphysics in Science.*
[2] This does not imply that all science is necessarily and finally true, for the advance of science is itself a dialectical development. Cf. my *Hypothesis and Perception*, (London, 1970) Ch. XI, and 'Dialectic and Scientific Method' in *Idealistic Studies*, III, 1973.

'science' is not confined to empirical knowledge, or even to exact mathematical construction, it includes the reflective and speculative disciplines of dialectical metaphysics. Rational conceptual awareness, mind as such (though mind, as such, includes more than rational concepts) reveals itself as the essential principle immanent in the totality of the real. The necessary continuity between material nature and spiritual (i.e., conscious, conceptual and rational) mind ensures an identity as well as a significant distinction between them. There can be no unbridgeable gulf between thought and existence. The natural world is the necessary process of mind's own self-generation. The idea, the rational awareness or concept, of the universal principle of being is, therefore, not divorced from existence, but is immediate evidence of its reality.

It follows, secondly, from the dialectical conception of reality, that each and every finite entity, all contingent existences, are self-specifications of the universal and are forms in an hierarchical scale. In each and every one of them, therefore, the universal is immanent. Its reality is thus implicit in their existence and follows necessarily from the bare fact of their occurrence.

Finally and most obviously, the whole hierarchical scheme manifests the being of the universal essence. Each subordinate scale and each successive stage, *qua* phase in a scale, is proleptic evidence of the eventual and immanent outcome—the final consummation, which is final in both senses of ultimate and teleological, yet, as we have shown, is not simply final, but also comprehensive and total.

These are the consequences of the dialectical conception and if the universe is a dialectical system, these consequences follow of necessity. But, it may be asked, *is* the universe a system of this kind? The answer is that if it were not it would not ultimately be intelligible, and if not ultimately intelligible then not intelligible at all (for reasons already given). But we have a conception of the universe which is in some degree intelligible, and intelligible structure is (as I have tried to demonstrate) inevitably dialectical. Therefore, the concepts of the world we already have are instances and evidences of its dialectical structure, without which we could not even entertain them. To state this otherwise, the world must be a dialectical system, for, unless it were, no coherent account could be given of our knowledge of it, and hence no account of its own nature whatsoever—we could not even entertain the supposition that it had some other form.

We may now consider the effect of dialectical reasoning upon proofs of the existence of God. Formal logic, whether traditional or modern, rests, as we have seen, upon the assumption that the world is a collection of finite particulars, the aggregation of which is infinite, if at all, because it goes on endlessly. However impressive the conception of God might be, on this assumption, He would be no more than one particular among others, set beyond the aggregate which makes up nature and therefore, like all other individual entities, finite. His existence, if he exists, would be inevitably contingent and could not be necessary. It could not be necessarily involved in any conception of him. The Ontological Proof couched in terms of traditional logic must therefore be invalid. It seeks to prove a conclusion which conflicts with the presupposition of the logic by which it seeks to prove it. And if it could succeed it would only have proved the existence of that which could not be God.

The dialectical conception of the infinite, however, rules out the conception of God as a magnificent finite. God can be neither an unending collection of finite contingent beings nor another finite, however glorious, beyond temporal finites. He is and must be by nature and definition an absolutely infinite and necessary being—'that than which a greater cannot be conceived'.[1] In short God is the true infinite, the consummation of every dialectical scale. Dialectical logic, therefore, requires the reality of God as the ground and foundation of all finite being and of all reasoning: of all finite being, because God is that ultimate essence or principle immanent in every finite, without which (as Spinoza says) it can neither be nor be conceived; of all reasoning, because all reasoning is the self-development in

[1] Note that this definition is never appropriate to the deity conceived by the finite understanding.

consciousness of the concrete universal, which realizes itself in consciousness as the principle immanent in nature through which conscious beings have been generated. These two forms of immanence are only apparently two. They are really two aspects of one immanent self-expression. It follows at once that God cannot be conceived except as existing, that his essence involves existence—not simply his own but all existence—and the Ontological Proof is vindicated.

The same metaphysical truth validates the Cosmological and the Teleological proofs, which, for similar reasons to those given above, are invalid on the assumptions, and if stated in the framework, of formal logic. The series of finite causes to which the understanding appeals to explain transient events is endlessly finite. It can encompass no ultimate explanation of any existence, and no valid transition can be made from it to a 'first uncaused cause' existing of necessity. Not merely, as Kant showed, is this attempted transition a tacit appeal to the ontological argument, but even if it could be made it would not account for the finite series of causes. A necessarily existent transcendent being is not of itself an efficient cause of finite events and is imagined to be one only if thought of as an anthropomorphic God who creates a world *ex nihilo,* as a human artificer might construct an artefact out of given material. There is no obvious way of deducing an endless series of finite causes and effects from a self-subsistent, uncaused, necessary being. As *causa sui,* and because it is *causa sui,* it must be self-complete and so in need of nothing either to bring it into being or to augment its nature. In that case nothing should issue from it as additional to it. Whence, then, proceeds the endless succession of finite causes of which the uncaused cause is supposed to be the ultimate source? What exists by its own nature alone is an infinite being, and nothing else is thus self-existent. And such an infinite cannot be a mere summation of finites, because finites cannot be infinitely summed into a true infinite. Any aggregate of finites remains finite, hence the problem of accounting in terms of efficient causation alone for finite existences. The true infinite, however, is completely self-sufficient and all-inclusive, for anything excluded from it would be a limitation of it rendering it finite. It cannot therefore exist apart as the uncaused cause of subsequent finite effects. The assumption of an uncaused cause which is in this way antecedent to a train of subsequent effects is a self-contradictory idea, because, so separated from its effects, it would not be infinite and so could not be *causa sui*. God conceived in this way by the understanding is not truly God, and the Cosmological Proof in the form framed according to the logic of the understanding involves an illegitimate leap from the spurious infinite to the true infinite, which leaves obscure the very explanation of finite existence that it seeks to establish.

Dialectically, on the other hand, nothing exists which is not a specification of the immanent self-differentiating totality. The manifest existence of any finite, therefore, is a presented instance of the universal principle which, when dialectically developed issues in and reveals the nature of the whole. The dialectical progression is not a regress *in infinitum,* but a development necessarily culminating in the true infinite. It requires, therefore, that from any finite existence the implicit existence of God must be dialectically deducible. In dialectical logic the Cosmological Proof is therefore valid.

Similarly, for the finite understanding, order is simply a special arrangement of otherwise independent and self-subsistent particulars. It could come about by accident, or it may be brought about through deliberate disposal of the elements by an intelligent agent. If it is accidental it proves the existence of no supreme being. If not, the questions remain, what constitutes order in nature and whether the appearance to us of an orderly setting is indeed what it seems to be. Moreover, the requisite order is asserted to be teleological and the purpose it serves is not demonstrable. The arguments of Spinoza and Hume to this effect are devastating and need not be repeated.

But if all relations are, as we have contended, features of a structured continuum, and all arrangements of parts in consequence systematic; if every system is a scale of forms and every scale dialectical, as we have maintained; then the teleological character of the real is inescapable—not in the sense that everything serves a purpose (whether man's or God's) but in the sense that the nature of every finite being, the occurrence of every finite event, and the explanation of every finite complex, depends upon the whole to which it belongs and in which it occurs. The universal organic principle that constitutes and is the infinite whole informs and determines every detail. Accordingly we cannot doubt that there is order in the world—for order and structured form are prior to the elements which constitute it. Those elements are nothing but the self-differentiations of the concrete universal. They manifest its principle and give unshakable proof of its reality.

Dialectical logic thus establishes the existence of God in all those ways in which formal logic fails to do so. The traditional proofs are implicitly the expression of that metaphysical truth which is the foundation of all thought, all reasoning, and all consciousness as well as of all existence. They fail only when expressed in forms inappropriate and incompetent to achieve the truth which they nevertheless strive to establish. But their failure neither abolishes nor merely relegates to uncomprehending belief the conviction of God's reality. It makes way for the rational demonstration through dialectical thinking of the inescapable presence and ubiquity of God's being as the irrefutable foundation of religious faith.

Theism is not, therefore, a matter of mere faith rationally unsupportable. It is a matter of knowledge; and Spinoza was not being pretentious or merely arrogant when he wrote to de Burgh that he knew he understood the true philosophy as de Burgh knew that the internal angles of a triangle equalled two right angles. The true philosophy for Spinoza was the knowledge of God and was identified by him with true religion. It was, moreover, not mere imagination, or even simply 'ratio', but knowledge of God by the third kind of knowing, *scientia intuitiva*, knowledge in the best sense. It is belief rationally justified and understood through the conception of the concrete universal, the true infinite, which is through its own nature *causa sui*. The denial of the existence of this infinite being leads ultimately to incoherence, incomprehension and self-stultification.

But what formal logic does not approve seems to the understanding either paradoxical or incomprehensible. Theories like Spinoza's or Hegel's which rest, implicitly[1] or explicitly on dialectical thinking are therefore rejected by the finite understanding as nonsensical,[2] or patronized as unscientific and mystical. Mysticism, however, is something different. It claims an illuminating vision of ultimate truth which dispenses altogether with rational support. That, indeed, gives the mystic a feeling of exaltation and redemption akin to Spinoza's *amor intellectualis Dei*, but is not, like it, the emotional counterpart of the highest kind of knowledge, for revelation without reason, though it may be belief, is not properly knowledge at all.

The God thus known is what Pascal decried as 'the God of the philosophers', the sort of God conceived by Plato, Aristotle and Plotinus, not, Pascal averred, the God of Abraham, Isaac and Jacob. In this he was so far right that the rational knowledge of God is, and can only be, metaphysical knowledge. Nevertheless, though religion relies on faith, that faith is not groundless nor irrational. Its rational support is given by metaphysics, so that the concept of God which is rationally established is a metaphysical concept. Hitherto, as is common in metaphysics, we have treated it only in principle and in general. We have referred to God only as a principle or Universal essence. This does not disqualify our conception or our proof from acceptance by the religious devotee. The conception of divinity can and must be still further developed to discover whether its implications do not in fact coincide with those of the dogmata of practised religion. If they do Pascal's contempt for the God of the philosophers and his reverence for the patriarchal God are ill-inspired. The idea of God current in biblical times, the tribal deity of Abraham, Isaac and Jacob, is hardly adequate to the theological conceptions of more developed religion and it would be wiser to reject that than to belittle the philosophical doctrine.

[1] Cf. my *Salvation from Despair* (The Hague, 1973), p. 125ff., and *passim*.

[2] Cf. Hans Reichenbach, *The Rise of Scientific Philosophy* (Los Angeles, 1957).

CHAPTER V

THE IDEA OF GOD

I

Every attempt to conceive the real as restricted within finite limits either explicitly or by implication denies itself and impels our thought beyond all limits to the postulation of an infinite being, on which all else depends and in which everything lives, moves and has its being. There must be, as Spinoza insisted, an infinite whole—call it what you will—in which alone anything can be, and through which alone anything can be conceived. It is in this inescapable fact that all the traditional proofs of God's existence are rooted. They maintain in effect, first, that the fact *is* inescapable (the Ontological Proof); secondly, that the finite nature of the world as we experience it, and of ourselves, as we know ourselves, makes the fact inescapable (the Cosmological Proof) and, finally, that whatever is intelligible is so only by virtue of its supplementation and amplification into that infinite whole, of which its intelligible structure is evidence (the Teleological Proof). It is one ultimate fact, and only one, that all three forms taken by the traditional proofs of the existence of God explicate and demonstrate.

What kind of concept can and must we entertain of this infinite being? That we can and must conceive of it somehow is what we have already established. But it must be immediately obvious that we can frame no complete and detailed idea of an infinite whole without ourselves being infinite and omniscient. If then we must form some conception of God, what conception is possible and what is legitimate?

The God whose existence is proved by the traditional arguments has been called 'the God of the Philosophers' and has been scorned and reviled (especially by Nietzsche) as such. It is the metaphysical conception of God which, alone, seems susceptible of any proof, and this has been decried as a cold theoretical entity towards which nobody could possibly feel reverence or devotion. It is, so the criticism alleges, a passionless inhuman entity with which no personal relations could ever be established, to which no prayer could be addressed and of which worship would be either idolatrous or absurd. A merely abstract, theoretical concept would indeed be subject to all these strictures and limitations—and for that very reason could be no legitimate concept of God; but Nietzsche and the critics make no consistent attempt to replace what they deride by any more acceptable conception. They conclude too readily that none is possible, yet to reject every idea of God is to leave even their own doctrine, so far as it has positive content, truncated and incomplete. The concept of God cannot be abandoned without abandoning all coherent theory.

The concept of God entertained, however, cannot be abstract, for God is the *ens realissimum,* the most complete, the most perfect being, and so must be conceived in the most concrete manner possible. The content of the concept is the fullest and most complex. Nothing less could in any way answer to reality. It is, of course, metaphysical, but only misguided prejudice assigns to metaphysics the most abstract concepts—one which identifies, quite falsely, universality with abstraction. The opposite is the case; the most universal concept is the most concrete and that is the typical and most appropriate subject matter of metaphysics. Aristotle made no mistake when he identified Metaphysics with Theology, the science that comes after and goes beyond Physics.

That the concept of God is metaphysical, however, by no means precludes its object from the sphere of religion or renders it inappropriate to worship and to love. *Dei intellectualis amor* is a religious emotion. In fact, most other concepts of God are inappropriate for religious devotion, and prove on examination to be idols. Even when religious fervour is sincere its object (through the ignorance of the devotees) may be misconceived. The tribal god of the ancient Hebrews was hardly less of an idol than those of their enemies, and 'Jehovah thundering out of Zion' is scarcely an appropriate object of enlightened religious devotion. The representations of God in finite forms which have been used by religious sects in the past are almost all of them unacceptable as true representations, as are many that are still adopted. But, on the other hand, it would be rash to reject them all out of hand, for religion presents its object in symbolic forms, and symbols are unavoidably finite configurations, not to be confused with what they symbolize. When they are so confused, God is misconceived and true religion degenerates into idolatry.

Nevertheless, religion has many forms and faces. It is cult as well as concept. It involves practice as well as belief. And what religion sets out in imaginative form may well be (in fact, almost invariably is) a representation at some more or less undeveloped stage, of what emerges under criticism as a metaphysical concept. The God of the philosophers, therefore, so far from being a mere abstraction, is not unrelated to the God of religion, but, on the contrary, results from the attempt to make religion intelligible. It is this attempt that is expressed by Anselm in his confession, 'Credo ut intelligam', and, in as much as it succeeds, the conception it attains is what Hegel called the truth of religion.

How, then, are we to conceive the infinite being towards which the inevitable self-transcendence of the finite points? The natural answer would surely be given by tracing out the tendency of each of the forms of self-transcendence which we discovered in Chapter III, to see whither it tends in each case and to determine whether the direction of the nisus in each example converges with the others towards a single end.

II

First we found that knowledge in science involved transcendence of the finite because the subject of that knowledge could not consistently be brought under the laws and categories by which all its objects were determined. That which transcends the merely finite object of a science of finite entities subject to causal laws is consciousness, and, especially self-consciousness— consciousness of self as the subject of scientific knowledge. The sheer objectivity of science proves incompatible with the sheer subjectivity of consciousness. Reflection upon scientific knowledge finds these two aspects of knowledge to be mutually necessary and correlative and at the same time mutually irreducible. Some philosophers have tried to reduce the objective world to ideal content, but in so doing they reveal yet again, and in a new way, the transcendence of the finite by consciousness. For this reduction (what Husserl terms 'transcendental reduction') makes the knowledge of the world the intentional object of a transcendental subject, which can in no consistent manner be made part of the world which it knows. It cannot be identified with any finite self or psyche without paralogism,[1] and its purview becomes inevitably all-inclusive and potentially infinite.

The trend of this line of reflection is towards omniscience and reveals essentially a conscious subject, self-aware in its awareness of all else. The critical point of reflection at which this revelation dawns is that at which the finite mind seeks its own identity and finds that it cannot deny its own existence or abjure its own subjectivity. It is the self-discovery of the *cogito* and its inescapable noema (what Husserl calls 'absolute consciousness'). The infinite thus immanent in human knowledge is a consciousness, a knowing, an infinite intellect. Whatever deity is indicated by this mode of reflection is a self-conscious, omniscient deity—an absolute subject of an absolute knowledge.

III

Not only science as the knowledge of nature, but also nature as discovered and envisaged by science, when we reflect upon it philosophically and seek to make our ideas of its parts and phenomena consistent, transcends finite limits and prefigures an infinite being. This, we found, was the implication of an evolutionary conception of natural forms; for no relationship between forms and no process from one stage to the next is properly evolutionary unless the second involves and includes the first,

---

[1] Cf. my paper 'The Problem of Self-constitution in Idealism and Phenomenology' in *Idealistic Studies,* Vol. VII, 1977.

and at the same time exceeds it in the degree of adequacy with which some principle of organization is realized—a principle already immanent and operative in the earlier stage. Such a relationship must be essentially dialectical; that is, the principle of organization (or unity in and through differences) must be immanent at every stage, must progressively realize itself more fully throughout the process, and will be such as can be completely manifested only in a totality in every detail and in every aspect wholly actualized. It follows that each phase and every entity in which the immanent principle reveals itself is a whole of some sort and holds potentially in its nature the forms that can evolve from it. The process from one such whole to the next, more articulated and more integral (and concomitantly more versatile) whole is one of sublation (*Aufhebung*), so that the subsequent form, while it transcends its predecessor, more fully explicates what, in its predecessor, was coming to fruition. The most fully developed manifestation of the principle, therefore, most adequately reveals the character of the universally immanent principle and is that which gives clearest indication of its true nature.

Organization we found typical of, inherent in and prior to, every natural form; and organization essentially implies ultimate completeness, self-closure and self-determination. There can be no such thing as an ultimately incomplete or incurably partial structure. For the fragmentary character is recognizable as a structural part only in terms of the whole, and only by virtue of its wholeness can structure exist. The tendency throughout the gamut of natural forms from physical to biological and thence to psychological is continuously towards more complex, more integral and more self-determining wholes and thus moves inevitably in the direction of total completeness or absolute wholeness. The spatio-temporal universe conceived (as it is in modern physics) as a definite yet boundless extension is the initial manifestation of this trend. Within this are microcosms; the interlocked totality of energy fields determining the structure of the atom, molecular patterns, the leptocosms of crystalline form, and the almost inexhaustibly complex wholeness of the living organism. But at each specific level there is one totality. First there is the physical whole just mentioned; next the biosphere incorporating all life into one organic whole; finally the noosphere, the world comprehended in the system of knowledge. Pantheism is thus ruled out, for nature transcends itself, towards a totality not simply natural, but, as mind, essentially supernatural. Its totality is sublated ideally in an infinite spiritual whole which is prefigured in its own natural product, the mind of man.

IV

The unity of the whole is sublated in, as well as presupposed by, the unity and reflective self-consciousness of human personality. A passage from Pierre Teilhard de Chardin gives apt expression to this fact;

> 'The more one heeds the invitations to analyse urged on one by contemporary thought and science, the more one feels imprisoned in the network of Cosmic inter-relationships. Through criticism of knowledge, the subject becomes continually more closely identified with the most distant reaches of the universe, which it can know only by becoming to some degree one body with it. Through biology (descriptive, historical and experimental), the living being becomes more and more in series with the whole web of the biosphere. Through physics, a boundless homogeneity and solidarity is brought to light in layers of matter. "Everything holds together" . . . . The world constitutes a whole.'[1]

Thus is the whole of nature brought to consciousness in our minds, through the process of nature; and the wholeness of nature, with our own integration in its unity, made apparent to us through reflections upon our own consciousness of nature. At the same time we are acutely aware of our inability to do full justice in knowledge either to its wholeness or to its detail. Sim-

[1] *Christianity and Evolution* (London, 1971), p. 100.

ilarly, our concomitant accomplishments in moral, social and artistic activity, even at their most spectacular, impress us with their failures, and we can never deem ourselves to have realized the potentialities of the whole. At the same time our awareness of our own shortcoming is the measure of our self-transcendence. As we saw, 'the greatness of man is great in that he knows himself to be miserable'. Man infinitely transcends man just at the point where nature transcends nature.

The natural series issues in human personality, with that characteristic awareness of its own deficiencies and limitations which Pascal recognized as the very insignia of its self-transcendence, and which is at once the incentive to aspiration towards perfection and the well-spring of its yearning for atonement with, and absorption in, an infinite divinity.

The clue to the conception of deity thus afforded lies both in and beyond human personality. It is neither fault nor wonder that man in his religions tends to conceive God in his own image, or, what is in effect the same thing, believe himself created in God's image. For human personality is, even to itself, recognizably incomplete, inadequate and partial, pointing to its own transcendence in an infinite, perfected personality. Such infinitely perfect personality is, of course, difficult (one may well say, for us, impossible) clearly to conceive, yet it is something which we cannot avoid conceiving because it is inexorably involved in our own nature and in all nature. An infinitely perfect personality can obviously not be entirely like our own, yet the whole trend of natural evolution guarantees that the infinity immanent in it cannot be less than personal, it cannot be non-personal, it cannot be *impersonal* and still adequate to the explanation of what develops within the natural sequence. To call it supra-personal would be more appropriate, but would scarcely make the conception more intelligible. So it is apparent why anthropomorphism in religion, while up to a point natural and even inevitable, is nevertheless inadequate and productive of misguided superstitions.

V

The idea of personality is by no means simple or clear even
as applicable to men. It is one we freely and frequently employ
but seldom understand or clearly articulate. Nevertheless, certain
indispensable features of it can be distinguished without great
risk of error. Undoubtedly it involves self-consciousness, and the
conclusion that we reached above, of absolute subjectivity as
characteristic of deity, is entirely consistent with it. But the conditions in which self-consciousness can arise even in ourselves
are very complex and require examination. The natural emergence of consciousness of any kind presupposes a developed organism, and in human kind this development has reached a high
degree. But the isolated organism is certainly not all that is involved. In fact, no organism is isolated, for every organism is an
open system in unceasing, intimate, organic interrelation with
its environment—an environment to which no ultimate limit
can properly be prescribed. The organism is a microcosmic reflection or registration of effects from the entire universe (as,
in fact, according to its degree of evolution, is every natural
being), and in consciousness this registration of the whole comes
to awareness of itself. But such awareness has to be engendered
and fostered in conditions provided by spontaneous as well as
passive reactivity, and by social intercourse with other conscious
beings. Further, merely immediate consciousness is not the highest phase of our experience. Reflection and systematic thinking
supervene, and without them knowledge, in the full sense, art
and religion, those forms of experience in which transcendence
beyond the finite is most evident, could not emerge. But reflection and systematic thinking are the products of education,
which is a social process. Accordingly developed mind is inseparable from social organisation.

In the first place consciousness of self develops only in cor-
relation with consciousness of other. Intersubjectivity is a condition both of objective knowledge (for the antithesis of subject
and object implies the publicity of the object) and of personal
self-awareness. There is no personality without inter-personal

converse. In practical terms, as Marx understood, this presupposes the supply of material needs and economic inter-relations. Society grows up from these roots, and interpersonal commerce generates moral obligation. But this can occur only at a level of thinking which is in some degree reflective. It implies deliberate social organization, from division of labour for subsistence to specialization of function in complex institutions. Its foundation is reason, which is the universal source and principle of order; and of that, again, the indispensable condition is submission to law. Here is the source of social obligation, the external imposition of which by government is impracticable without the support of self-control and self-discipline on the part of the members of the society involved. In the final analysis, therefore, subjection to law always involves self-subjection. Social and moral conduct are always action in accordance with the *idea* of law. It is thus, in the last resort, self-determination, and Kant's insight is vindicated that freedom is obedience to the moral law.

Just as no organism can be isolated and remain alive, so no person can realize his or her personal capacities in solitude. All knowledge is a social product, not alone because it requires education of the younger by the already learned for its acquisition, but also because its advancement and retention is maintained only through discussion and the intercourse of minds. Without knowledge and some degree of intelligence there can be no deliberate co-operation for material production. Again, physical welfare can be assured only through social co-operation, and the achievement of moral aims only on the basis and through the realization of social welfare. Without all this, again, political freedom must remain imperfect and at best an unattained objective. These are all conditions of happiness, without some conception of which (be it pleasure, or salvation) there is no intelligible moral end. So the moral law, we must conclude, is equally a social product. Moreover, moral freedom, like morality in general, depends on that capacity for reflection and self-awareness which can develop only in a civilized community. Without such capacity even the more radical freedom, to which Sartre and the Existentialists lay claim, is inconceivable. In fine, personality is always social. Whatever the individual is, he is in society; to be himself he must transcend himself; to realize his personality he must realize the idea of the community in which alone he can be himself. In no other way can personality be brought to its perfection.

But the perfection is an ideal never fully realized in ordinary human life and society. The moral perfection that it represents goes beyond that of 'my station and its duties', displays itself in dedicated service, self-giving and finally as religious devotion, and the exhortation appropriate to it is that of the sermon on the mount;

> 'Be ye therefore perfect, as your Father in Heaven is perfect'.

As personality involves society and the practical endeavour to fulfil the highest aspiration must be made in and through community, its projection—its self-transcendence—is envisioned as 'the Kingdom of God'. The perfection of moral personality, therefore, involves religious community, a Church, in which the members constitute the body and the Deity the head; and in this communion the service of God is perfect freedom.

In all this we see not only the vindication of Kant's moral teaching but also in some measure, that of Marx's social doctrine. But because in all of it the finite constantly transcends its own limits, the community in which personal freedom is realizable cannot remain a purely secular society. The secular outlook is the outlook of the finite individual who retains self-interest as his goal, failing to identify it wholly with the communal interest. The communistic demand is for this ultimate identification; but the communistic contradiction is to imagine that the demand can be fully met at the secular level. The incentive to meet the demand remains, at the secular level, self-interest, and when that is eliminated no incentive operates. Only when the incentive becomes a religious aspiration and a devotion to a transcendent ideal can the demand be adequately satisfied. That is why the ultimate community must be a religious community and the ultimate ideal the Kingdom of God. That communism should have some contribution to offer towards its realization is not improbable. Aristotle and Plato taught that friends have all things in common; and the early Christian Church gave the same injunction to its members. For Christ had said to his disciples, 'I call you not servants; for the servant knoweth not what his lord doeth; but I have called you friends. . . .'

However that may be, the point at which our reflection has now arrived is that God is the transcendent moral ideal and the Kingdom of God the transcendent ideal of society. We found earlier that finite humanity, in and through social and personal morality, without which man is neither civilized nor properly human, transcends itself, and is conditional upon an aspiration towards infinite perfection. This, in imagination, is clothed in the images of human immortality and divine goodness. Now again we find that the conception of deity is to be approached through extrapolation of the notions of moral perfection and social harmony.

Here, however, we are faced with a dilemma. Must deity be conceived as embracing the entire spiritual community, or is it to be attributed only to its titular head? And what, in any case, is the relation between ruler and subjects in the divine commonwealth?

The Christian Church represents itself as the body of Christ of which all believers are members, and Christ is the head. This suggests that the relation between man and God is analogous to that of the cells in a living body (say the phagocytes in the human organism) to its mind. Lewis Thomas suggests a similar relationship between the ant and the ant-hill (with its queen), and the bee and the hive.[1] He repeatedly hints that man's relation to the earth is not dissimilar. Perhaps, adapting Rupert Brooke, we might think of ourselves each as 'a pulse in the eternal life'. But if God were conceived as a vast organism, in which we were 'cells', there must be enormous differences in the mutual relationship. Phagocytes, or ants, or bees, are not self-conscious minds. They are not persons; nor is the hill or the hive; and

[1] Cf. *The Lives of a Cell*, (New York, 1974)

men are not conversant with their own phagocytes. A human community is very different. There is a sense in which it has a mind of its own, common to all its members because of their conscious participation in common activities. It is a mind, not separate from those of its members, but constituted by their several contributions to the co-operative thinking. Each of the members is aware of the thought of all the rest to the extent that they co-operate with him and he with them. In a human community, the leaders have (or at least can have) personal relations with their followers, but in a symbiosis there is no such personal relation between the symbiont and the coenosis. The image of a church permits of such relations between the persons of the members and of the terrestrial head; but that, though in some ways it may be analogous, falls far short of the relation between man and God.

Personal relations within a community, however, so far from excluding, presuppose and are dependent upon unity at more primitive levels. The union of saints in the body of Christ is conceived by Teilhard as a physical union. Discussing the Pauline pleroma, he speaks of Christ and the elect as 'forming one living whole', and of the beatific vision as '*a collective* act performed by the whole mystical organism' (his italics). Grace, he says, 'brings with it a certain progressive inclusion in a created organism, physically centered on the humanity of Christ'.[1] Teilhard's precise meaning is difficult to grasp; but the idea is certainly worth pursuing. The unity of the universe has already impressed itself on our minds, and the intimate inter-dependence of all natural forms. In all of them we have found the whole immanent—a whole which is not merely material, but which transcends even the organic. What seems undeniable is that no breach can occur between God and the world. All is one indivisible series in which the lesser and lower is wholly dependent on the consummation, and in which the consummation is the result of the development of the lower—not its temporal effect, but the eternal actualization of all that is potential in the incompletely developed. This unity and continuity applies equally to

[1] *Op. cit.*, pp. 16–17.

the upper strata, where mind has come to consciousness and spirit is aware of itself as such. The unity of man and God in Christ is the essence of Christianity, but that of Christ and his Church is no mere physical, nor even an organic unity. It is one which sublates all physical and biological nature, as well as mental, aesthetic and moral experience, in one transcendent spiritual whole.

Our argument hitherto has established the immanence of infinite being in the mind and consciousness of men. God is what makes all minds intelligent and all things intelligible. Equally all benevolence is response to the prompting of a transcendent ideal, and all beauty the actualization, in its appropriate form and degree, of a transcendent vision. The ultimate source, and at the same time the ultimate goal, of this inspiration is the absolute spiritual whole, and it is in terms of integration within that whole that man's relationship to God is to be conceived. That we cannot conceive it with full clarity is only to be expected, for absolute spirit in its infinity, while necessarily immanent in all experience, so far outstrips our limited capacities that it blinds us by its very effulgence.

Nevertheless, we may at least be sure that in such integration of finite minds within the divine personality no true individuality is lost, for the essential being of the ultimate whole is to be a whole of differences, each contributing its own special and peculiar character and tribute, complementary to every other. The concreteness of the reconciliation and combination of these differences is the greater, the more sharply their initial divergence seems to oppose them to one another. What at finite levels issues as conflict and disharmony becomes, when its implicit tendencies are developed and corrected, cooperation and concord. The wayward desires of men conflict among themselves and defeat their own end of self-realization, until through self-awareness and reflection they are mutually adjusted and subordinated to a moral ideal. The actions of men bring them into conflict, until by the same means they become aware of their common interest and govern their conduct subject to a social ideal. But no moral or social ideal is adequate short of divine perfection.[1] That must be realized (as it is already immanent in all human endeavour) in a supra-personal divinity in which the diversity of human personalities are harmonized in subordination to the integrating principle of the whole—the ordering and co-ordinating governance of divine wisdom.

How is the reality of this supreme perfection to be conceived? First, it is immanent in the experienced world; secondly it is immanent in man's aspirations and endeavours towards the perfection of himself and his society. But in these it is still only potential. It is the dialectical relation of the continuous scale of phases in nature and in human development that compels us to postulate and affirm the reality of the consummation. It is not, as we have already conceded, a fully actualized object of our finite experience and could not be. But the actual consummation is an indispensable condition of the existence of the whole, as of any part, of the scale, and so of our experience itself. The grounds which we have explored above support our belief in its reality, the belief which is religious faith in its most genuine and legitimate form, 'the substance of things hoped for, the evidence of things not seen'.

In denying that God could ever be an object of finite human experience Kant was certainly correct. In asserting that the Absolute is immanent in all things and thus, as finite spirit, becomes progressively more fully aware of itself, Hegel more perspicaciously grasped the truth. God becomes the object of man's worship and the goal of his self-transcendence because God is the indwelling spirit of all nature, from which man has evolved, and of all human awareness itself in the whole scale of its achievements, in Spinoza's words, 'from the highest to the lowest grade of perfection'. In the face of the ubiquitous evidence we cannot deny the existence of God, but in 'our benumbed conceiving' we do not comprehend him.

[1] See below pp. 117, 130 and especially 154.

VI

Let us now try to summarise results. By following the trends of transcendence disclosed in the nature of the finite, we project the infinite as an absolutely self-complete whole comprehending and continuous with all finite nature, realizing itself progressively through natural processes, in which (consequently) it is immanent, and eternally actualized as a self-conscious infinite super-personality. The transcendence of knowledge, as the subjective apprehension of an objective world, issues similarly in an infinite subject intending an infinite object. The actualization of both these aspects also encompasses complete moral and aesthetic perfection as it involves a community of persons with a single ultimate aim. God is thus in dim forecast to be conceived as an infinite, omniscient, selfconscious, spiritual being, actualizing the potencies of physical and biological nature, supra-personal in character and including in his single unity a multiplicity of spirits—a kingdom of ends, an integral union of all minds in one transcendent individuality. The various aspects of deity are not separable from one another, any more than deity itself is separable from the hierarchy of finite forms. There is nothing abstract in this conception—quite the contrary. It is not even remote, although it is certainly transcendent; for what the Absolute transcends is still itself, its own primitive phases. *They* are, each in its own way, abstract; and it is their abstraction that the divine consummation overcomes and remedies. Hence we are not cut off from the Godhead, but are constantly, though in varying degrees, in communion with the divine.

The conception of God adumbrated above includes the traditional attributes of omniscience and supreme benevolence, but no emphasis has so far been placed upon omnipotence. There is, nevertheless, a sense in which that too is implicit. It is not the sense (if it is at all legitimate) in which omnipotence means ability to do anything whatever. It is the sense in which, through universal immanence of the infinite, whatever is done is a divine act and whatever can be done (and only that) is 'the will of God'. To allege otherwise[1] is not to enhance but to diminish the divine power, because it implies that God's action might somehow fall short of his full concreteness and bring about some effect in isolation from that solidarity and density of interconnection which the real unity of things in God involves. From the point of view of the infinite everything is as it must be and occurs as it should and this is no derogation of God's freedom, for in all his activity he is absolutely self-determined. And at the higher level all activity is spiritual, though that, as we have seen, cannot be divorced from the finite phases which it sublates and through which it realizes itself. Spiritual activity, in its self-awareness and consequent self-specification, is wholly free and constitutes the freedom of the phases of activity which it sublates, for their determinism is its determination of them, the exertion of its freedom as the totality which is immanent in their (which is its own) specificity. On the other hand, the totality is not a fixed scaffolding supporting a separable canopy. It is an activity, a perpetual dynamism of successive phases of self-realization; and these phases are gradations of lesser and greater wholeness, or degrees of perfection. Consequently, there is a sense in which what is and occurs at lower levels is not as God wills, is not as it should be, and is not wholly free. It attains a greater measure of freedom at the next higher level, which is more what it should be; and it does so through the immanence in it of the totality—which is 'God's will'. From the point of view of the finite, therefore, there is evil and defect and a perpetual struggle to overcome them.

The admission, even from the finite point of view, of the presence of evil in the scheme of things raises the most serious question concerning the notion of deity, and is the source of the strongest objection, and the one most frequently raised, against belief in God. This and related questions remain to be considered and may not be overlooked. In the face of the ubiquitous occurrence of evil, can the conception of God so far outlined reasonably be maintained? If it can, what is to be said of sin

[1] To suggest, for instance, that God could have created some other possible universe.

and redemption? How are they compatible with it? Does it, and
the relation it implies between God and man, admit of prayer,
in any intelligible sense, or any inter-personal converse between
finite and infinite? These are closely related questions which
cannot easily be separated. Obviously, the problem of evil involves and includes the nature of sin and how and whether it
can be expiated. Prayer and intercession are mostly concerned
with these matters. They are almost always related to sin and
evil, as deprecation of transgression and supplication for perfection, as repentance for wrong-doing and petition for forgiveness,
or as thanksgiving for deliverance and hope of future safety. The
last merges into praise of God as the expression of atonement
and beatitude at the final triumph over adversity and subjugation of vice. Adequate discussion of such difficult topics can
hardly be accomplished in a paragraph and some attempt to
cope with them follows in succeeding chapters.

Chapter VI

EVIL AND TRANSFIGURATION

I

The problem of evil is the most difficult confronting the theist, and the existence of evil has always been cited by atheists as the most persuasive fact in support of their disbelief. How, it has been demanded, can evil in any form be thought compatible with divine goodness, omniscience and omnipotence? If everything that happens is in any sense God's act, if all reality and occurrence is the effect of God's power and will, he must be the ultimate cause of all error and evil, the reality of which none can plausibly deny. How, then, can God be at once omnipotent and benevolent?

The objection has recently been reiterated by Professor Brand Blanshard in his latest book, *Reason and Belief*. The problem of evil he finds an insurmountable obstacle to a rational belief in God, and its treatment by theology he considers 'an intellectual disgrace'.[1] The question at issue, he claims, is straightforward and demands a straightforward answer. It is the question how the actual amount and distribution of evil in the world can be reconciled with its government by a God who is in our sense good. Professor Blanshard presumably includes omnipotence in the conception of Godhead, for the question is different and less difficult to answer (as Hume and J. S. Mill recognized) if a deity less than omnipotent is contemplated. The arguments that have been offered all break down so notoriously and so promptly, Blanshard maintains, that theologians take refuge in blind faith or revolt against reason altogether. Their appeal most frequently is to the inscrutability of God's will, which amounts to much the same thing, and incidentally implies an ultimate irrationality in God, not only by our standards, but by any standard that would render the universe an intelligible

[1] *Reason and Belief* (Yale University Press, 1975), p. 546.

whole. Accordingly Professor Blanshard concludes that the reality of evil—which he does not doubt and considers undeniable—is irreconcilable with benevolent divinity; but not, it seems, with a coherent universe lacking any such divinity.

The intelligibility of the world for Blanshard consists in its being 'an order in which all events are interconnected by links of causation and necessity',[1] but it is not a system which 'can be described with self-evidence as a mind or conscious',[2] although minds emerge within it, and values arise in relation to the impulses and desires experienced by conscious beings. It follows for Blanshard, that the universe at large cannot have value, the conditions of which are known to be realized in only a very small part. That the world is a single causal system necessitated in every detail is an assumption which, he holds, we are justified in making because without it we should have no pretext for seeking to understand—no incentive for the quest for knowledge—but it does not follow that the universe itself is ratiocinative. Much less does it follow that it satisfies our moral or aesthetic interests, for these aim at creating an ideal object not yet existing, as opposed to the intellectual interest in discovering and comprehending one already there.

This conception of a rational world is more nearly akin to that envisaged by the understanding than by dialectical reason, although it differs from the empiricist view in holding causal connections to be necessary and ubiquitous. It also differs markedly from the view outlined above in Chapter IV, and whether it could be maintained without generating internal inconsistencies is a matter requiring further investigation that would divert us from our present object.[3]

The attempts, which Blanshard castigates, to reconcile the presence of evil in the world with a benevolent deity are all attempts made at the level of the understanding, and, for the most part, they are associated with a finite and inappropriate

---

[1] *Op. cit.*, p. 510

[2] *Ibid.* and p. 524

[3] See, however, my paper, 'Rationalism and Reason', forthcoming.

(sometimes even ludicrous) conception of God. It is no wonder that they are spectacular failures. Those he lists are (i) that evil is introduced into the universe only by man's free will, and became general through original sin, (ii) that it is offered to test our faith or to strengthen our moral character, (iii) that it is not real but is only an illusion of our minds, (iv) that 'it represents some inexplicable impotencies (unfortunately conjured up *ad hoc*) in the divine power',[1] and so on. Nine of these ploys taken by itself will serve, nor all of them together in Blanshard's system, or in most of those he criticizes. But, as I shall try to show, a dialectical conception of reality and thought can accommodate some form of each of them, and can offer a solution of the main problem, though whether Blanshard would consider it a straightforward answer to what is, after all, not so straightforward a question as he avers, is far from likely. But before I do that, let me make some preliminary observations.

II

Good and evil are for the most part human evaluations made in relation to human wants and feelings. They are, in consequence, inconstant and diverse, often producing incompatible judgements. Many theorists have been led by this familiar variability and contradiction among recognized values to maintain that good and evil are purely relative, not only to one another, but also to circumstance, opinion and habituation. If this were the final pronouncement on the matter, the problem of evil for theism could not arise; for if good and evil were purely relative forms, in the way alleged, they would not be real in any strict or relevant sense. If what one cherishes another deplores and neither can be independently good or evil, these terms cannot properly be used as names to designate or describe definite entities. The existence of evil would then become a meaningless phrase and the terms good and evil would be inapplicable to the nature of things conceived as created by an omniscient God. To omniscience nothing is merely relative: everything simply is.

[1] loc. cit.

If good and evil were merely relative to human feeling, to omniscience they would be simple facts without evaluative qualities.
On such a view God himself could not be adjudged benevolent
or malicious, and human malice could not be condemned or
adversity lamented as positive evils. Such judgements would be
merely particular, relative to the person's sentiment who made
them, and could never be objective or of universal validity. The
allegation of incompatibility between evil and omnipotence
would consequently fall away. It is curious that the objection
against theism based on the presence of evil in the world is most
frequently brought by philosophers (though Blanshard is not
one of these) who also hold the view that all value judgements
are non-cognitive and that standards are purely relative, a view
that must render their objection meaningless.[1]

What is relative in any sustainable sense must be relative to
some standard or absolute criterion, an implication that rela-
tivists ignore. Nevertheless, relativism is not wholly false for
human sentiments and judgements do vary and fluctuate. They
are vitiated by limited knowledge and the confusion of vision
attendant upon man's finite nature. Once this is recognized
moreover, we may be wary of accepting human evaluations as
ultimate. What we consider evil may not be so by standards
which, because of our limitations, we cannot understand or
appreciate. It is rash, therefore, to declare that no benevolent
and omnipotent God could consistently permit conditions which
we consider evil by our varying and conflicting standards. If our
confused opinions are submitted to criticism and corrected, if
our judgements could be more fully informed and our insights
deepened, our views of good and evil might be so transformed
that the entire issue of theism in relation to values would be
altered.

---

[1] Cf. my *Revelation through Reason*, Ch. VI, pp. 100–103.

III

To make consistent sense of radical relativism, however, is a hopeless task and the most reluctant are constrained to adopt some absolute standard of value. As often as not (or more so) the standards assumed are pleasure and pain, but they cannot be maintained. The arguments against hedonism are many and familiar, and in the final assessment they are unassailable. Aristotle made clear twenty centuries ago that pleasure supervenes only upon successful activity, and no activity can be successful unless it attains its end.[1] That, accordingly cannot be pleasure, for the attainment of the end is a prior condition to enjoyment. But it is the aim and end of action that is identified as the good, and failure to achieve it as evil. These cannot be pleasure and pain for they are only consequent respectively upon attainment and failure.

The criticism of hedonism by T. H. Green is a repetition and elaboration of Aristotle's. It is meticulous and detailed and along with Bradley's is conclusive. Their arguments need not be repeated, though they have been too long ignored and too easily forgotten.[2] Moreover there are others which must convince us that pain and evil are not to be identified, even if often they happen to coincide. Both pain and pleasure have ambiguous reference. They refer to physical sensations as well as to emotional qualities, and in neither case can they be identified with good and evil. The physical sensations serve biological functions without which the higher forms of life could not survive. Pain warns the sentient organism of dangers that it must avoid to escape destruction. Children born incapable of feeling pain so far from enjoying greater good, are in constant peril of physical damage and death. Pain must, therefore, be valued as a good so far as it serves an indispensable biological function. The suggestion made by John Stuart Mill, and others, that sufficient avoidance of harm could have been assured simply by the pursuit of pleasure, is fallacious. For pleasure and pain *are* mutually

[1] See *Nicomachean Ethics*, 1174b, 1175a.
[2] Cf. T. H. Green, *Prolegomena to Ethics*, Book IV; F. H. Bradley, *Ethical Studies*, Ch. III.

relative. The absence of pleasure is felt as pain and the relief
of pain as pleasure.[1] The enjoyment of pleasure is never wholly
exclusive of pain, and, in certain circumstances, sensations of
pain are even found to be pleasant. Not only so, but if pleasure
could be enjoyed without correlative pain, its exclusive enjoyment would be biologically disadvantageous, for the obsessive
pursuit of pleasure leads to the neglect of more essential needs
contributing to health and satisfactory living. A rat trained by
neurophysiologists to press a key, which stimulates, through an
implanted electrode, the pleasure centre in its own brain, neglects the search for good and risks starvation and death. The
supply of essentials involves effort and some degree of discomfort, while it is notorious that overindulgence in pleasure begets
illness and physical deterioration.

The argument is frequently put forward, that even if man,
with his free-will and consequent propensities to evil-doing, had
never appeared on earth, evil would still exist in the pain and
suffering of animals. The struggle for survival which evolution
requires involves, it is maintained, the most savage and ruthless
destruction of living things, the privation and death of the
weaker thrust aside by the stronger in competition for the means
of survival. But this imagined conflict is not at all what contemporary biologists view as the reality. Tennyson's image of
nature 'red in tooth and claw with ravin' has long been rejected.
In the first place, as we have seen, pain and fear serve a beneficent function in preserving the individual creature from harm
and so assist in its survival. But apart from that quite general
consideration, we must distinguish between pain as a physical
sensation and pain as consciously suffered. It can only be experienced as a conscious distress if more than mere sensation is
involved, for sensation is unreflective, and one sensation follows
upon another, each ceasing as the next begins. To be aware of
sensations, whether pleasant or painful, a conscious subject must
be able to relate them as successive, each as passing and the
next as coming to be, which involves a persistent subject of
awareness that cannot be identified with any one of its transient

[1] Cf. Plato. *Phaedo,* 60B.

feelings, nor even with all of them as a mere succession or collection. They must be cognized as a series or order and must be felt as objects. In fact, something very like a conscious self or *ego* is a condition of suffering as something more than a mere passing sensation. At most only the higher animals attain to this level of consciousness, even if sentience may be present lower in the scale than we suspect.

Even among the higher animals, however, such consciousness as they enjoy is unreflective. Unlike men, they do not 'look before and after and sigh for what is not'. They are wholly absorbed in instinctive behaviour which is entirely extrovert and so, for the most part, and especially under the influence of fear, unconscious of present pain. Even men acting under stress and in excitement (for instance in a battle) become aware of any hurt that they may suffer only after the action is accomplished and time for rest and reflection is available. Accordingly, biologists assure us that the natural life of animals in the wild is active, rhythmic and care-free excluding functionless pain and terror. It is man's interference that causes needless suffering to wild and domestic beasts so far as they are capable of experiencing it.

In human life, on the other hand, pain and evil are far from being universally identified. Even in common experience we do not always regard pain as evil. Many games, which we enjoy even to the point almost of fanaticism, involve extreme exertion and considerable discomfort. We value and greatly admire, as spectacular achievements, exploits involving great danger and severe hardship, like Hillary's conquest of Everest or Chichester's circumnavigation of the earth; and we should shun, as the extreme of boredom and dullness, a life of indolent ease and perpetual effortless comfort. Beyond biological fact and sporting aspiration, it is still more significant that many people have succeeded in converting suffering, even in extreme forms, into a stepping-stone to contentment and beatitude—more than have found salvation in a life of self-indulgence.[1]

[1] Cf. *Revelation through Reason*, pp. 106–111.

The identification of pleasure with good and pain with evil is thus quite unjustifiable. Pleasure and pain are terms designating agreeable and disagreeable feelings associated with physical sensations and emotional states, they are not evaluative terms. Good and evil are epithets indicating opposites on a scale of values. In certain ways they do involve pleasure and pain but are by no means identifiable with them. In fact pleasure is sometimes good, sometimes a concomitant of the attainment of good and sometimes the very opposite of good, and the relation of pain to evil is similar. The tacit identification of pain with evil in arguments about the incompatibility of evil with divine benevolence, therefore, simply confuse the issue. For there is no necessary conflict between omniscient benevolence and the occurrence of pain among sentient beings and it is only when and because pain happens to be evil that it becomes relevant to the question under discussion.

Nevertheless, there are innumerable cases of intense pain occasioned and suffered needlessly without any apparent countervailing benefit. There is frequent pain and suffering unjustly inflicted and futilely undergone. Whatever might be the mitigating considerations, surely (many will contend) such suffering is intrinsically evil, and to those who experience it unqualifiedly real. How can such evil be wiped out by other and irrelevant enjoyments? Just as pleasures cannot be summed in experience as a single sensation, pains cannot be balanced or neutralized by disparate pleasures; and, if some pains can be integrated into larger experiences which are on the whole valuable, this seems hardly true of all suffering. None of these contentions can (or need) be denied; yet (we shall shortly see) in accordance with the conception of an infinite God as consummation of a dialectical scale of developing finites, even the reality of such evils can be seen as compatible with the perfection of deity.

IV

Blanshard is so far right that good and evil are conditional upon desire; not that what is good is always desired or what is evil always shunned, but that apart from desire nothing would ever be evaluated. It follows that only for consciousness and reflection are objects either good or bad. Instinct and appetite imply attraction and aversion, but only when self-awareness converts these into felt desires are their objects valued. Even then, it is strictly only contrast and comparison between attractive and repulsive objects that properly gives rise to evaluation. Value is inseparably bound up with choice and that implies preference between alternatives. Conscious distinction and comparison are therefore indispensable to it. The universe contains value, therefore, only so far as it contains conscious minds, and if as a whole it has value it can be only for conscious minds.

Preference and choice between alternatives, distinction and comparison of objects require judgement, and all these are the ingredients of free volition. Whatever conclusion one may adopt about the freedom or unfreedom of the human will, one may state unreservedly that there could be no free will without conscious purpose and deliberate choice. If our will is free it is and can be so only because, and only so far as, we are aware of our ends and choose the means to them by rational deliberation. The concomitance of value with consciousness, purpose and deliberate choice gives colour, therefore, to the contention that evil (and we must surely include good as well) is introduced into the world solely by man's free choice. Indeed the strict and proper use of the terms 'good' and 'evil' has moral reference only. Other uses are derivative, secondary and often (if not always) illegitimate. To substantiate this statement here would be too lengthy a digression,[1] but we may note that it is supported by Socrates' and the Stoics' doctrine that what is evil is not the suffering of pain and injustice; it is to commit injustice and to inflict unmerited harm upon others. It is man's moral action that is good or evil, not his fortune or misadventure.

Evil is a very comprehensive concept. It is the negative of whatever is the goal of legitimate endeavour, of everything

[1] A carpenter or a tennis player is 'good' so far as his skill conduces to success, but success in special pursuits is itself good only so far as it contributes to the goodness of life as a whole, and that in the final issue is the moral end.

rightly held to be good. This statement admittedly begs questions, but they concern the definition of the good and we may pass them over here. That which conflicts with whatever good may be is what is meant by evil. Thus if knowledge is an ultimate value, ignorance and error will be evil; if physical well-being is good, disease and decreptitude are evil, if virtue and righteousness are good, vice and wickedness are evil, if beauty is to be sought as an ultimate desirable, ugliness in every shape and form is evil. Yet there is a sense in which all values are subordinate to moral value for every good is the object of desire, and desire can be satisfied only through action, even if it be no more than the acceptance or rejection of a gift. All action, properly so called, is deliberate and purposive and its purpose must be estimated according to its contribution to and compatibility with the structure of the good life as a whole: that which ultimately satisfies the total self. It is this assessment that determines its goodness or badness in the last resort; and this assessment is a moral judgement.

Evil, then, is primarily what affects the moral character adversely and, if Aristotle is to be followed, what affects the character either well or ill can only be practice and the habit of choice. Suffering, however hard to withstand, adversely affects our moral action only so far as we freely choose. The harder the choice the more creditable the virtuous action, and failure under duress is excusable just to the extent that freedom is attenuated. In that case it is not altogether untrue that the 'evil' of suffering and pain 'is sent to try us' and to strengthen our moral character. We achieve good by withstanding and overcoming it; and we succeed in doing so the more easily when we recognize that to regard suffering and pain as evil in themselves is a misapprehension, and that nothing is bad without qualification except a bad will and a guilty conscience.

True evil, therefore, is human malevolence, the possibility of which is necessarily entailed in freedom of choice. It has been argued therefore that evil cannot be avoided if freedom is to be ensured and that a world without free and moral agents would be immeasurably worse and poorer than the actual world with all its crimes. Clearly this is true so far as freedom involves self-consciousness and *vice versa*, for a world in which self-consciousness was not achieved would (if possible at all) be lacking in every form of value. Whether it would be possible at all is a point to which we shall return, and, if it is not, the presence of evil in the world is no obstacle to belief in the existence of an omniscient, omnipotent and benevolent God, because it is no limitation upon power to be unable to bring about the impossible.

A counter to this argument has been offered by Antony Flew and others who have alleged that men could quite conceivably have been created both free and unfailingly virtuous. The choice of evil, they say, is not necessarily involved in freedom. Clearly it is possible always freely to choose rightly, and a race so constantly virtuous would establish what believers call the Kingdom of God. But, like all moral good, the Kingdom of God cannot be imposed upon men by force or fiat. It has to be won, against odds and is realized only if it is attained by man's own effort, willing aspiration and choice between alternatives. It must be sought, at least initially, through human endeavour, requiring moral education progress and persistent striving. A race of men directed from without, made constitutionally incapable of evil choice, or (as Flew in one place seems to advocate)[1] under a sort of hypnotic compulsion towards beneficent action, would be neither free nor moral, and in what sense their behaviour would be 'good' is not apparent. They could not be citizens in any ideal state and would fall as far short of moral perfection as the inmates of Aldous Huxley's Brave New World.

Moral attainment is a result: the outcome of a progression, the issue of a development. It is not something (as Aristotle so rightly saw) that can be possessed without training and constant practice. The reason for this is that moral conduct is the regulation and government of natural impulses to achieve what Plato called a harmony in the soul. The conflict of inherent tendencies in men frustrates their satisfaction as intelligent beings, and the

[1] Cf. *New Essays in Philosophical Theology* (London, 1955), 8, pp. 144–69.

channelling and rational ordering of their natural propensities is both the beginning and the continuing theme of morality. The insistence of instinctive urges presents a constant pressure and temptation to self-indulgence which is the root of vice. Man as a natural being can never be free of this temptation, and his animal nature is inseparable from his moral character. The doctrine of original sin, therefore, though it may present difficulties to some philosophers in its theological form, is not impossible of coherent rational interpretation.[1] The suggestion that the presence of evil in the world is attributable to man's free will and is perpetuated by original sin is far from senseless and can consistently be accommodated by a dialectical conception of the nature of reality and of perfection. For in that conception nature is the prior phase of the dialectical progression, the dialectical opposite, yet the inevitable origin of mind, which is immanent in all natural forms and actualizes in spiritual activity the potentialities of nature.

No such possibility is recognized by Blanshard, who sees the dependence of value upon human consciousness as in conflict with the allegation that an intelligible universe might itself be valuable or conscious. For the universe, he holds, is not self-evidently a conscious mind and although our conscious minds emerge within it, the rational form that we attribute to the whole satisfies only our intellectual demands but neither our moral nor our aesthetic. Were the universe no more than a causal system such as he describes it would indeed not self-evidently be a consciousness. Rather it would be the direct contrary. Nor could it possibly satisfy our moral and aesthetic quests, and it is more than doubtful whether our intellect could rest in a conception so obviously problematical. Neither Kant, who generated the Antinomies out of precisely this type of world-view, nor Plato's Socrates of the *Phaedo* thought that it could. But if the causal system (however comprehensive and reciprocally complete), which is projected as the goal of scientific investigation at a certain level, is at best an abstract view

[1] Cf. W. G. Maclagan's discussion in *The Theological Frontier of Ethics* (London, 1961.), Ch. II.

of a more concrete reality, a reality that is a teleological and dialectical whole, the case is very different.

In a dialectical system, consciousness and mind are higher phases in a scale, the lower phases of which, its dialectical progenitors, constitute inanimate and animate nature. Mind then should be the fuller expression and more adequate manifestation of the universal principle differentiating itself as the entire scale; and thought, the peculiar activity of mind, would be the principle immanent in every phase and developing itself throughout. The nisus of the development would be towards that form of perfection in which conscious thought finds its fulfilment; and, in that, intellectual, moral and aesthetic satisfaction would ultimately be inseparable. That this is so will be self-evident to one who realizes that conflict between moral and aesthetic ends frustrates the intellect as surely as it must frustrate both moral and aesthetic aspirations. Nor can any sheerly irrational end ever really satisfy our moral intuitions. Again, elegance of demonstration is as much a requirement of intellectual perfection as it is of aesthetic taste. Ultimate fulfilment must be a single ideal and cannot, if it is ultimately to satisfy, be fragmented. Such a dialectical system, then, would necessarily culminate (as has been argued above) in a consciousness, supra-personal in form, in which all the highest values are realized together and in one.

It is in the context of such a system that we must seek the solution of our problem, which is not one of explaining how some finite but insuperably powerful creator of a correlatively finite world could be regarded as supremely good if he permitted evil to occur within the world. This image is full of contradictions and is rightly rejected. We have seen that God and his relation to the natural world can and must be differently conceived in a coherent philosophical theology. Our problem is perhaps more difficult and far less straight-forward. It is how the perfection in which the dialectical system culminates can be identified with the whole process and yet tolerate or even require imperfection in its temporal phases; how evil which actually occurs can be cancelled out. Though it may possibly be corrected, remedied and superseded, how can evil that has

once occurred be totally annulled? How is it conceivable for a
perfected intellect and supra-personal morally ideal individual
to countenance concomitant evil or to expunge the blemish of
past committal?

v

Milton writing of

> '. . . man's first disobedience and the fruit
> Of that forbidden tree whose mortal taste
> Brought death into this world and all our woe'

has his priorities right. Evil is first man's dereliction consequent
upon his knowledge of good and evil—his awareness and free
will—and only after that death and all our woe. Death and
disaster are, however, most frequently cited as the impediments
to belief in a God of justice and mercy. Biologically, however,
death is an evolutionary achievement, the condition of sexual
reproduction, the development of which has made possible evolutionary advance beyond the vegetative to locomotive and
appetitive levels of life and eventually to the human and intelligent. The lowest forms of life do not die. Their cells divide
and recapitulate their youth in continual renewal. Only the
higher species die, which reproduce through sexual differentiation and copulation. The meiosis and refertilization thus involved distribute and combine divergent genes in so enormous
a variety of permutations that evolution of new species and
adaptive advance is immeasurably facilitated. Sexual reproduction requires segregation of somatic from reproductive cells, so
that the latter are virtually immortal while the former decline
and die. Here then Milton (knowing little science) has gone
astray. It is not the fruit of the forbidden tree whose mortal
taste brought death into this world, but death that has made
possible the eventual evolution of conscious intelligence and has
brought into this world creatures capable of knowledge and so
of choice and 'disobedience'.

The fear of death, as we have earlier intimated, also serves
a biological function, so far as it helps preserve the individual

by instigating action to escape from danger, prolonging life sufficiently for continued reproduction and the propagation of the species. But death is to be feared, prevented and deplored only for the sake of other ends which have intrinsic value. So far as it prevents their achievement it is undesirable, but in itself it has no taint of evil. Interminable life in terrestrial circumstances is far from being an alluring prospect, for the very nature and conditions of life make perpetual youth a contradiction and continuous aging an increasing tribulation. Longings for immortality are due to an imaginative confusion between unending life and eternal blessedness, the former being interminably finite, immersed in temporal change and process, but the latter being altogether independent of time in the apprehension of the transcendent infinite.

Perhaps some may reply that the tedium and decrepitude of old age is itself an evil that remains uncompensated. But that complaint again confuses pain with evil and overlooks the facts that old age and decline are the counterparts and conditions of youth and regeneration. More important is the fact that age is not necessarily mere senility. It brings with it tolerance, wisdom and balanced judgement easing the violence and asperity of youthful reactions. A life-cycle is a whole: youth, maturity and age, to which each phase is integral, and as a whole it is itself a phase of a larger whole in relation to which it must be judged and understood.

If death is at worst derivatively evil; major catastrophes are to be similarly assessed. Floods, earthquakes and volcanic eruptions are no evils and are not even thought to be so unless they destroy human life or its necessities. But human life is inherently destructible and the only attendant evil is the extinction of potentialities. That men are destroyed by natural cataclysms is no malevolence of nature and no worse, if more dramatic, than the effects of disease or death. The whole conduct of life consists in the surmounting of difficulties and threats intrinsic to natural processes, and its failures are but the consequences of its finitude. Natural disasters, in fine, are misadventures and they are

not the source of evil. Good and bad are qualities attaching to
the ways in which human beings respond to them, not to the
natural occurrences themselves. Accordingly, the destruction of
human life by natural upheavals is no more a reproach to God
than it is to nature. It is largely irrelevant to the main issue,
which is directly concerned, not with the processes of inanimate
nature, but with the attainments (moral and spiritual) of the
human soul. God's goodness is not measured by his protection
of men from danger or the distribution of good fortune, but by
the maturation of man's own moral consciousness and his ability
through spiritual magnanimity to triumph over natural ills. To
these the goodness of God proves an ever-present aid and perpetual support, in ways which we shall explicate anon.

The most formidable barrier to the conquest of evil, or any
theory of the supremacy of good is man's own atrocity. The
wanton and ruthless cruelty, the unscrupulous exploitation and
the insidious treacheries of man are evils that cannot be argued
away. The perpetrated horrors of Auschwitz and Buchenwald
and the devilry of Dostoevsky's general, who deliberately set his
hunting dogs to pursue and tear to pieces a naked child in revenge for a thoughtless and boyish prank,[1] are evils which seem
unexpungeable from the make-up and the history of the world.
What future good could compensate for such depravities? How
could they be ever justified as means to ulterior ends? Or what
redress could ever be made, or penance ever served, to expiate
their vileness?

Our moral susceptibilities are so shocked by these enormities
that they appear to be absolutely evil without the least tolerable
component, and we recoil from any cold dispassionate analysis.
But when we force ourselves to closer scrutiny, we find that even
here there is a positive aspect of the committed acts which makes
them in some sense redeemable. Spinoza taught that evil was
purely negative, mere privation of what, if added, would convert
it into good. The positive aspect of an immoral act, he maintained, taken simply on its own merits contained nothing evil.[2]

---

[1] *The Brothers Karamazov*, Bk. V, Ch. IV.
[2] Cf. *Epistle* XXIII.

The examples given above seem at first blush to contradict this view and to be evil in a more positive sense, inexplicable merely as privation of good. Even these, however, more carefully examined, turn out to be mere privations, the incidents of defective reality the positive elements in which are not reprehensible. The kind of analysis that would show this in detail would require a book-length study of its own. Here only the barest indication can be given of what is meant.

The cold-blooded callousness and cruelty of these hideous acts is in part the outcome of emotions and sentiments which have been distorted, confused and deflected from their normal expression. In themselves and in their normal form they are not evil and could equally have been the causes of virtuous acts. The diabolical pleasure taken by sadists in the pain and suffering of others is, at least in part, a distortion of sexual cathexes which if normally satisfied would be beneficial. That these natural urges should have been so distorted is, of course, itself deplorable; but the causes of that again are found to be influences in themselves directed towards desirable ends. As Freud has shown the conditions of social order require the repression of certain instinctive urges and this is frequently brought about in ways that give rise to neuroses issuing in abnormal and anti-social forms. Hitler's paranoia was in all probability a case in point.

The Nazi enormities, however, were not merely expressions of aberrant emotions. They were highly organized societal activities requiring high intelligence and technical skills. These too, in themselves, and properly exercised, were capacities for social order and co-operative action. They were misdirected capabilities for good. Thus extreme viciousness was the outcome of the corruption of faculties in themselves potentially of the highest value. What turned their course awry was their diremption from their proper context, not the introduction of any positive element of evil.

What then of the appalling suffering of the victims of Belsen and the Nazi death camps? The truly evil aspect of that is its infliction upon them by their captors. The degree of misery felt by each cannot be judged by other individuals, and no sum of sufferings can be made by combining the torments of different sentient beings. That six million victims suffer makes little difference to the suffering of each one, except perhaps so far as the awareness that others are equal victims might make the endurance easier for some individuals. The moral significance of suffering, as has been said before, depends upon the reaction of the victim. If he or she endures with fortitude and patience, pain is transmuted into glorious martyrdom. There must have been countless acts of selflessness and courage among the inmates of Nazi concentration camps. Their heroism is no plea in mitigation of their murderers' guilt, but it wholly transfigures the misery of their torture.

The character and action of Dostoevsky's general would be another instance of deformed emotion and distorted instinct, which in their normal states would not be evil. Even so his ferocity and sternness, directed against a worthier and more legitimate opponent, say some dangerous miscreant, would be appropriate and admirable *in itself,* and apart from its misdirection, it is nothing ill. In fact, in its worst aspect it is the defect of a finite personality prone to misdirection, excess of feeling and expression, passionate folly and uncomprehending lust.

But the point of the story is not so much to condemn the arrogance and cruelty of the perpetrator as to deprecate the suffering of the child and his parents. Of the latter we can say again what has been said of the victims of Buchenwald, and the pain and terror of the child, though horrifying to us who contemplate it, to him, in his innocence and inexperience, would, similar to that of a hunted beast, have been much less and more short-lived than that of the sympathetic adult witness. Consciousness, in such a case, is so obsessed with immediate action that sensation is largely anaesthetized and speedy death puts an end to all pain. Pain and suffering always involve some measure of self-awareness and self-pity, which must be absent from the consciousness of a hunted animal obsessed with the strain and effort to escape. Once again, no such consideration justifies, excuses or condones the act of cruelty. But what in it is positive is not evil. The child's fear is a protective instinctive urge, his flight a salutary reaction. The dog's behaviour is purely natural and amoral, and our own horror at the thought of the event is the measure of our humanity and loving-kindness. The evil of the incident is actual and terrible, but it is not a positive reality. It is a disruption or shortcoming in a limited entity (e.g., the character of the perpetrator), potentially good in its positive constituents, but made evil by their aberration and misdirection from the proper course of action. It is this intrinsic relativity of evil and the finiteness of its subject that give the clue to the solution of our problem.

VI

The factors which constitute an action or situation either combine harmoniously or are brought into conflict. In the first case the action or state of affairs is good in the second evil. All human conduct, which is the proper subject of the evaluative epithets is an endeavour to secure satisfaction through the harmonious exercise of capacities and gratification of compatible desires. The endeavour goes astray when desires conflict and impulses are turned awry, when capacities are misused and propensities exaggerated. In all such cases disharmony results both in society and in the individual personalities affected. This is the form of evil, but it is also the spur and pretext for reform and the dynamic of further endeavour. Without conflict and frustration there would be no effort to improve; without pain and evil there would be no progress to a better condition. But in no action or endeavour of finite beings is success ever total, and the standard by which it must be judged is a condition of the self in a way of life which as a whole gives the greatest satisfaction. Good and evil as adjudged in actual cases, therefore, are always relative to this proximate standard, are never in practice absolute, but are always a matter of more and less.

What is bad in relation to the better may be good in relation to the worse. It is this fact that has in part led thinkers to de-

clare all value judgements relative. Further, even those goods
which have been called 'intrinsic' like health, honour and virtue
are ranged in a scale of degrees in which some are subordinated
to others. Again, as judgements are man-made, they differ from
one society to another as well as among individuals. But this
does not justify relativism as the final account of value, because
much of this relativity (as we noted) is consequent upon the
limitations of human insight, and that again is a matter of
degree. A scale of degrees, however, whether of goodness or of
wisdom, implies an absolute standard to which they are relative
and by which they are measured. The lesser degrees are all
gradations of finiteness, and the absolute is the sublation and
the truth of all finites. The scale of values is thus part and parcel
of that dialectical process earlier described, in which, without
the finite and apart from the scale of degrees, there is no consummation and could be none. Because it is the sublation of all
finites and all lesser degrees, the consummation is not merely
the end but is the whole, process and end in one. And because
it is the sublation of all finite phases and nothing less, without
the scale of degrees neither could there be nor be conceived
any perfection. The conceiving is itself the immanence of the
whole in the lower phase (the mind of man).

Evil is incident upon finiteness, as we have observed even
in Dostoevsky's horrifying example. It is, in fact, the very badge
and consequence of defect. It is therefore a necessary feature of
the lower phases of the scale through which perfection is generated. If this were not so there would be no dynamic pressure
in the direction of improvement, for the dialectic of contradiction and conflict, in which evil is involved, provides the main-
spring and the stimulant of progress. Similarly there would be
no ultimate realization. The whole, we have insisted, is no
abstract, separable end-state. But (as Hegel constantly averred)
it is a result—the completion of a perennial process of self-
realization. If it were otherwise it could not be a *concrete* self-
differentiating whole and would be less than perfect. There is
no such thing as perfection (in the true sense of that word)

which is merely abstract and separate from the process of realization.[1]

All evil, therefore, is necessary evil, even when it seems otherwise to us, for we see only as through a glass darkly, only from the viewpoint of a certain grade of finitude. To us our own pain and suffering may seem unqualifiedly evil. Yet only a little reflection has revealed the error of that belief. The nature of evil and the ultimacy of its reality are complex subjects which cannot here be adequately investigated; but it does seem undeniable that, however, unmitigated evil may look to us, the process of the real is its continual overcoming, a continuous struggle to rise above it; not necessarily, if ever, by eliminating pain and discomfort altogether (the attempt to do that may well be misguided), for they, in certain settings may be necessary elements in the good; but through their transfiguration in the progressive sublation of the finite towards the ultimate realization of an absolute redemption.

At the appropriate levels of finiteness pain and evil certainly and inevitably do occur and are not unreal. But in another sense they are not real—in the sense that no finite, because it is finite, is fully real. Its reality and truth is in what it becomes through development and sublation in a fuller and higher reality, which remedies its defects, fulfils its wants and cancels its corruption. In a scale of forms, each advancing on its predecessor towards total completion, there is no absolute break, and the whole scale is one and indivisible. It is only when we think of it as spread out in time, and of time as divisible into separable parts that reconciliation between defective rudiment and perfected fulfilment presents a problem. But so to conceive the scale is to think pictorially and not conceptually. *Sub specie aeternitatis* its aspect is altogether transformed. Its phases are not separable and none are dispensable to the whole. The truth and the reality are, thus, the whole; and, in that, all evil is absorbed and cancelled. But

---

[1] Process must not be understood as purely temporal. There is also a necessary aspect in which, *qua* process, it constitutes an eternal whole eternally self-realized; for unless this were so, no process could be actually progressive.

this consummation cannot be without its lesser phases. Perfection cannot be realized without imperfection in the phases of its self-generation. So the idea of an absolutely benevolent and omnipotent God, who might create a world devoid of all evil, is an impossible abstraction, a fallacious and incoherent misconception.

Further, the needless suffering and futile pain which so obsesses our imagination is felt by finite subjects none of whom is self-complete. How their experience may be absorbed into one more comprehensive and how transformed in its fusion with what lies beyond it, we are unable to fathom. But we do have some clues to what may be possible and some indications, in hypnosis and yoga, of the power of the mind to obliterate and to overcome pain and suffering. And even where this does not occur, a more adequate understanding of the total situation might result in a very different evaluation from our common judgment, even of what seems to us to be wanton and purposeless misery. Thornton Wilder has striven to illustrate this possibility in *The Bridge of St. Luis Rey*.

Essential evil, moreover, is not pain but moral turpitude and that is neither more nor less than the incident of finiteness. Moral failure and weakness are most obviously privation and lack; and the deformation of feeling and action, which issues in what we tend to call 'positive' evil, is no less a consequence of limitation which truncates the personality and unbalances the emotional stresses within it. These distortions and disruptions are the chief causes of suffering not only to victims but also, in due course, to their oppressors. But they are degrees in a scale of continuous overcoming and sublation of finiteness, and so of evil—a scale which ranges from the worst to the better and from the better to the supremely perfect. Of this it cannot stop short, for every stage is a prefiguring, in some degree, of the standard by which each is valued, and without which there would be no scale—neither better nor worse. At the lower end are the miseries and the cruelties considered above, but, at higher levels, courage and devotion, virtue and endurance transmute suffering into triumph and victimization into heroism. Sacrifice may indeed be the very acme of attainment and the essence of salvation. The hero who gives his life for others comes, we are wont to say, to a glorious end, and the ultimate self-giving of Christ on the cross is the revelation of the way of love and of eternal life. The evil which is the occasion for martyrdom is the instrument of its own supersession, and the glory revealed in the sacrifice is the means of redemption for the crucifier himself.

The persistent critic will object that, even so, the evil incident upon the lower stages of the scale remains. Even though in higher forms it may be overcome, its marring of the lower is not remedied or compensated by what supervenes. But this is an error and a misunderstanding of the dialectical relationship. The finite forms, with their incident ills, become moments in the higher. They are sublated; that is, preserved and transmogrified, in a way which cancels their finiteness and annuls the evil aspect. The successive phases are not separable parts and the lower are not self-subsistent. A simple example of this is the human learning process in which mistakes are stepping-stones to truth, which we understand all the better for having previously erred. We grasp a philosophical insight more surely when we appreciate its refutation of an opinion we once held. Happiness is more truly found when one realizes that it is best attained only by abandoning the search. As the confessions of St. Augustine testify, the converted sinner is a greater saint than the ordinarily virtuous. These are, indeed, but partial and restricted examples which, at best, give only slight indications of the way in which error and evil are sublated in the truth and goodness that supersedes them, and how this is actually effected on the cosmic scale we can but surmise by analogy. Yet only a cosmic dialectic provides adequate explanation of finite structures and our conclusion follows from a universal application of its principle.

The sublation of finite forms in the complete realization of their potentialities must transform radically and completely what appears to us as evil. Just as the power of the intellect may transform the objects of emotion, so that when properly understood what once seemed threatening becomes no longer fearful, or what was once alluring no longer attracts, so the illumination of infinite insight into the wholeness and integration of all reality must dispel the shadows which, for us, obscure the truth and dismay the spirit. The infinite mind is of purer eyes than to behold evil, and the nearer the approach to infinitude the more completely does evil vanish by transmutation into the perfection of the whole.[1]

VII

The problem of sin and salvation is no different from the general problem of evil, and its solution is the same. The conscious realization, so far as it can be effected, by the finite mind of its union with the infinite, to which it already belongs and is already integral, is its liberation from the trammels of accidental evils, 'the slings and arrows of outrageous fortune', as well as from its own shortcomings.

Sin (as opposed to fortuitous ills) is the moral and spiritual failure attendant upon defect of intellect and will, the measure of man's finiteness and deficiency. It is spiritual failure, because it can occur only at the level of self-consciousness and reflection. The knowledge of good and evil is essential to it, the awareness of the imperatives of law and commandment. 'I had not known sin, but by the law', wrote Paul to the Romans, and again: 'we know that the law is spiritual, but I am carnal, sold under sin'. To be carnal is to be finite, and to be finite is to fail to live up to those standards that make spiritual demands. 'For that which I do I allow not: for what I would that I do not; but what I hate, that I do'.[2] Sin, then, is the inescapable accompaniment of finiteness, but the consciousness of it is the gateway and the goad to its transcendence. For it is 'what I hate' and 'the evil that I would not that I do'.

Apart from reflection, self-awareness and moral consciousness, there can be no sin. Evil there may be, but we should call it natural evil rather than vice. The behaviour of Freud's imagined primitive horde may be judged evil by more developed

[1] Cf. my discussion of Spinoza's theory in *Salvation from Despair*, Ch. VII, §7.
[2] *Romans* VIII, 7, 14–15.

standards, but (as has been argued) is not itself moral turpitude because it is purely instinctive. To sin man must have progressed beyond that level to one at which he is aware of his own wrong-doing, through an awareness of a standard of righteousness that is its measure. And that awareness, however inchoate, is the source at once of his sense of guilt and of his repentance. It is the rudiment of his salvation.

Accordingly, sin is the inevitable accompaniment of spiritual progress in a finite being. It is the mark of his finiteness, but also the point of transition towards the infinite. The theological conception of sin is that of rebellion against God and disobedience to his command and this is taken to be the origin and well-spring of all unrighteousness, all vice and all iniquity. Rebellion against God is self-aggrandizement or inordinate pride, and that is itself the product of reflection and self-awareness. But man's self-consciousness and capacity for reflective thought are precisely the 'image of God' in which theology assures us man was created. His rebellion, therefore, is but a defect or limitation of his potential infinity, a misdirection of his self-awareness which falls short of the infinity, of which it is a minute and subordinate part, and imagines itself to be the whole. It does so and can do so, however, only because the whole is immanent in the part, without which man's self-consciousness would be oblivious of its own transcendent potentiality. Sin, therefore, issues from man's very capacity for salvation without which he could never have transgressed.

The vice to which we are prompted by sin is the cause of conflict and strife between ourselves and our neighbours, as well as within our own personalities. But the conflicts arise in the pursuit of goods and interests which, on reflection, we find to be common. The end that satisfies must reconcile desires and interests and resolve conflicts, both within the individual and between individuals; and what truly fulfils either condition is found equally to fulfil the other. This end becomes the goal of our endeavour and that same standard which makes us aware of our own failings. Similarly it is this awareness that spurs us on to the effort to subdue our instinctive lusts and avarice, our envies and dissentions, and to seek that harmony and peace, both in society and in ourselves, without which we cannot rest. Our perpetual failure is, again, the consequence of our weakness and finiteness; but, as we have learnt already, man's misery and his awareness of his own failure is at the same time his greatness.

Sin, therefore, is not unmitigated evil, for it is both concomitant with spiritual enlightenment and the incentive to spiritual progress. Just as, without the transcendent potentiality of self-awareness there could be no sin, so also without sin there could be no spiritual attainment, for that is no more nor less than the achievement of those ends at which, in a perverted way, vicious desires aim. It is through the carnal alone and its self-frustration that we progress to higher aspirations. The satisfaction and peace which the world cannot give is to be found in the sublation, through the practice of virtue, of our carnal desires. But the practice of the highest civil virtue is not yet the complete attainment of righteousness which is to be 'perfect as your Father in heaven is perfect', and that involves something beyond mere human effort. Without sin there can be no redemption and redemption comes only through divine grace. Thus it is in religious devotion and worship that redemption is to be sought and there alone can it be found.

The essence of religion is the knowledge and love of God, the true infinite and absolute whole in which all finites are transcended and every conflict resolved. Such knowledge and love is incompatible with pride and inordinate self-inflation by the finite mind. It, therefore, eliminates and overcomes all sin. Such love and knowledge is no mere work of man and can be attained only by inspiration from the infinitude which is its source and object; for it issues from the infinite whole and cannot be a product of the merely finite. But the infinite with which the finite soul of man thus seeks atonement is not only transcendent; it is also immanent. It is not a mere perfection out beyond the finite; it is the actualization and consummation of all finite potentialities. Moreover it is actualized only through its own self-expression, self-manifestation and self-revelation in the finite grades and phases which constitute its systematic unity and wholeness and into which its unity is differentiated. These, therefore, with all their relative defects are as essential to its concrete wholeness as it is to their fulfilment and transcendence. They are taken up into and unified in its absolute completeness. Our finiteness is remedied in God only because atonement with God is neither more nor less than the fulfilment of our positive being and the complementation of our defect. The symbol of this translation of the finite into glory is the figure of Christ. It is only by the perfection in him of our imperfection and through our identification with him that our sinful selves can be redeemed.

Sin, accordingly, is the condition of redemption as well as the reason for its necessity; and salvation is the transfiguration of the finite not merely its supersession. In the transcendence which supervenes all evil is sublimated. Worship which is the medium of salvation embodies itself in good works and voices itself in prayer. Good works are actions done 'as unto the Lord', solely for the sake of actualizing in ourselves and others that perfection which is the knowledge and love of God. Prayer is communion with God; it is not a request addressed by finite man to a more powerful but still finite ruler. It is a search for and a submission to a higher consciousness, in which our own is sublated and absorbed and its immortal longings realized. We pray to be delivered from evil and diverted from temptation. Our prayer is the endeavour to purify our own minds through the consciousness of and devotion to that perfection which (through its immanence in them) they seek, and in which all defect is sublated and surpassed. The maintenance of that consciousness alone can save us from temptation and deliver us from evil. It delivers us from evil within ourselves by purifying our emotions and transforming self-seeking into love and charity towards neighbours. From external evils it delivers us by transforming our attitude towards them. When we come to see evil as the incident of finiteness and the condition of transcendence we no longer resent it. When we come to recognize good as nothing other than subjugation of evil in spiritual attainment and atonement with God, we no longer regard pain with unqualified repugnance, and the objects of our fears change. As we become aware of the internal conflicts in our own finite aims they lose their hold upon us and we are not led into temptation. The frustrations of our finite desires which we have hitherto regarded as misfortunes cease to distress us. Thus are we delivered from evil. As Spinoza has it: 'To the extent that we understand God to be the cause of pain, to that extent we rejoice'.[1]

Prayer in the form of confession and repentance is another aspect of this same spiritual catharsis. It sharpens the awareness of our own failure and directs our mental gaze upon the standard of perfection which makes that awareness possible. So in repentance we pledge ourselves anew to the endeavour of self-identification with the divine, and re-direct our minds towards the perfection of God. If we pray in the proper spirit and direct our minds to the proper objects so as to become effectively aware of the fulness and power of God's glory we are subjects of grace, the measure of the actualization in our persons of the immanent eternal.

Hymns of praise, verbalized frequently in inadequate symbols, are in essence the expression of the awareness and love of that infinite totality, communion with which we seek in religious devotion. So prayer in its diverse forms is the approach of the finite spirit to the infinite, the directing of the mind upon its true objective. But according to the measure of our intellectual grasp of its real nature, the language in which prayer is couched is more or less inadequate to its true meaning. It is always in some degree metaphorical, for our conception of the deity to which it is addressed inevitably falls short of complete comprehension.

Effort and concentration of intelligence, however, can bring us nearer to such comprehension. Superstition can be filtered out of our beliefs and in the light of the most rational and concrete thinking, we can arrive at an idea of God, consonant alike with science and morality, and internally consistent with itself. It is, as well, an idea that provides a basis for coherent interpretation of much traditional religious doctrine and practice. To expound and follow out such interpretation, however, would take us beyond the limits of this essay.

[1] *Ethics,* V, xviii, Schol.

CHAPTER VII

INCARNATION

'Furthermore it is necessary to everlasting salvation that he should also believe rightly the Incarnation of our Lord Jesus Christ.

'For the right faith is, that we believe and confess: that our Lord Jesus Christ, the Son of God, is God and man;

'God, of the substance of the Father, begotten before the worlds; and man, of the substance of his Mother, born in the world;

'Perfect God, and perfect man: of a reasonable soul and human flesh subsisting;

'Equal to the Father, as touching his Godhead, and inferior to the Father, as touching his manhood.

'Who although he be God and man yet he is not two, but one Christ;

'One, not by conversion of the Godhead into flesh but by taking of the manhood into God . . .'

I

Of the many traditional doctrines, for which the exposition set out above might serve as a groundwork for interpretation, the Christian dogma of the incarnation may seem most difficult, if at all possible, to accommodate. Yet if we are to find that teaching intelligible, and to regard it as more than a survival and adaptation of similar beliefs (of which there are many) among pagan religions, it should be capable of rational interpretation. To me this seems eminently possible, and without it religion is immeasurably the poorer and less adequate to human needs. Not only is such interpretation feasible, but it follows naturally and directly from the position so far stated.

The doctrine of the incarnation is aptly and succinctly stated in the lines of *Quicunque Vult* quoted at the head of this chapter; but it follows from what has already been set down that the phrase 'son of God' cannot be understood in the familiar biological sense of the words used. God, we have found, is the totality, and so is the eternal actualization of all potentialities, an activity which cannot be less than spiritual, self-conscious and supra-personal. Such biological implications as that may involve are only those of nature. Organisms beget other organisms in organic nature, but the totality does not beget other totalities. What it begets is the proliferation of natural forms. Apart from idolatry, therefore, if we speak of a son of God, we cannot intelligibly mean a para-biological descendant. The phrase can certainly be metaphorically applied to God's creation. A son is an immediate offspring who inherits the characteristics of his father; and Spinoza, in his *Short Treatise of God, Man and Human Welfare,* calls the eternal and infinite attributes and modes of Substance 'sons of God', because they are immediately derivative from God's infinite and eternal nature, and because they express God's essence more fully than anything else.

The notion of the Son of God, moreover, is messianic. 'Christ' means the anointed of the Lord, God's descent in finite form to bring redemption to mankind. That God should take the form of man seemed as ridiculous to Spinoza as that a circle should take the form of a square, but he 'thought far otherwise concerning that eternal son of God, that is, the eternal wisdom of God, which has manifested itself in all things, and especially in the human mind, and most of all in Christ Jesus'.[1] The Christ, the Lord's anointed, is the manifestation of God on earth in that human form which, as most fully expressing the wisdom of God, is the mediator between infinite God and finite man, and so the means of man's redemption. Christ is the redeemer. What ultimately redeems man from sin and evil, we argued above, is a constant and vivid awareness of, and participation in, the being and nature of God. Clearly, then, what redeems is, in a sense similar to that used by Spinoza, describable as the son of God. It is the idea of and devotion to God brought to full consciousness in the mind of man. The words of *Quicunque*

[1] *Epistle* LXXIII.

Vult are, accordingly, wholly appropriate to the relation between God and Christ. It is also entirely correct to insist that there is but one God, for it is the nature of God brought to consciousness that redeems and effects atonement with the infinite, and the medium of that atonement is the mediator—Christ.

Christ is God as redeemer; but redemption has neither significance nor relevance except for man, become aware of himself as finite, conscious of his own deficiencies, cognizant of good and evil, and so aware of a transcendent God. Redemption has meaning only in relation to sin and for those conscious of sinning. It is not relevant to lower nature, but only to 'fallen' man, to the Adam who has eaten of the tree of the knowledge of good and evil. God, the redeemer, therefore, is to be distinguished from God, the creator, although they are in essence one and the same, because the former is pertinent only to self-conscious human experience while the latter is the sublation, as well as the consummation of all finite being. The first has bearing only upon man as a moral agent with a moral sense, aware of an ideal and of obligation as well as failure to meet its demands. The second is the immanent and encompassing spirit of all reality. Yet they are both the same so far as the sublation of the finite is effected through a scale of forms which issues in human self-awareness, and the consummation is realized in human redemption.

That redemption, however, is the revelation to the sinful of the means of perfectibility of man in God. It is the revelation of the means of grace, which can be fully and effectively produced only by the actual presentation in fact of the objective unity of deity with humanity. Christ, accordingly must be both God and man—the God implicit in man's awareness of his own finiteness, brought to explicit realization as 'the propitiation for our sins'. Christ, the redeemer, is the manifest actualization of the potential for perfection in man through atonement with God. He is therefore God incarnate: 'God and man . . . is . . . one Christ'.

This union we must consider further, and particularly its historical occurrence in the ministry of Jesus.

If the argument so far developed is sound, there is a sense in which God is immanent in all human nature—a sense in which all are children of God, and so we are frequently described in the scriptures. There is no impassable gulf fixed between God and man. The unity of being has impressed itself upon us from whichever angle we have viewed it, and the very nature of God is to actualize himself in and as a gamut of graded forms, each and all of which are integral to his being and are sublated in his Godhead. Thus it is essential to deity to become incarnate. But, further, the immanence of totality comes to consciousness in man and makes him aware, as Pascal reminded us, of his own wretchedness. That again involves self-transcendence and the direction of the mind towards God. So far we already find God incarnate in all mankind. This is not yet redemption, but it is as essential to the divinity of Jesus as what still remains to be affirmed. Thus far we have but the germ and the condition of salvation without which Christ were but a voice crying in the wilderness. What is further required, however, is the revelation of the means of grace; and that is found in the personality, the teaching, the life and death of Jesus, as disclosed in the Gospels—the manifestation in historical actuality of human fulfilment through direct apprehension of God's perfection—God and man, one Christ.

Jesus is distinguished from other men by the fact that in his person, his conduct and his teaching, he revealed directly to mankind the nature and perfection of God. That he was a man is not subject to dispute; that he was God in the sense that God was immanent in his personality, as in all men, follows from our earlier discussion; that he expressed God's nature in superlative degree is evident from the Gospel record; that he was one substance with the Father must be immediately conceded so far as, in one sense, there is only one 'substance' and all men and all things are consubstantial in the final analysis. In another sense we may distinguish various grades of 'substance', and then Christ and God will be one substance in the highest degree, as has already been shown. In that he is saviour, Jesus is one with God; in that he is human, he is one with man; in that he is both, he is the union and atonement of human personality with the transcendent infinite.

> 'Who although he be God and man, yet he is not two but one Christ; One, not by conversion of the Godhead into flesh: but by taking of the manhood into God.'

All this is implicit in the conception of deity outlined in the preceding sections. The identification of Jesus as the man in whom the union is fully realized is all that remains to be established.

II

His claim does not rest upon virgin birth, which is strictly irrelevant, nor does it rest on miraculous deeds, nor on the resurrection of the physical body. Whatever may be the truth or symbolic import of these matters, Jesus' claim to unite God and man—to be the redeemer—is established solely by his personality, his teaching and his conduct. These (as I shall try to show below) leave little room for doubt or cavil, and apart from them the rest would fail to substantiate a claim to divinity.

The perfection of man is essentially a moral perfection, for artistic talent and intellectual acumen are gifts rather than virtues. Their potentiality for good or evil depends rather on how they are used than on their innate capacity. Morality is, of course, not separable from intelligence nor intellect from artistic taste and creation, for each infects both of the other two. All great art is morally inspired, even in the representation of evil, and intellect prostituted to immoral ends is both degenerate and self-stultifying. Accordingly, it is in moral insight and practice that we must seek to find the perfection of man, and it is in this form that it is revealed to us by the teaching and the person of Jesus. He presents to us in concrete form an ideal which appeals directly to our moral sentiments, but which can be sustained against criticisms (including those we have already examined) only by rational analysis. Its foundation, like that of all truth, is the self-conscious totality of being—in brief, God.

The *amor intellectualis Dei* is the perfection by which our Father in heaven is perfect, and to that Jesus exhorts us and, in his own practical life, he actualizes it objectively. This is the sole justification of the claim made for him of divinity, and other supports must be treated as symbolic or as legendary. But even if no such claim could be fully substantiated on historical grounds, the records which have come down to us, the beliefs which they have inspired about their central figure, and the actual effects they have had upon individuals and peoples, would establish the person of Jesus as the symbol of the Christ—the redeemer who must be at once God and man.

We may begin by considering the question whether historical grounds are either necessary or legitimate. It will be declared by some theologians that the divinity of Jesus is known to us by divine revelation, that the Gospels are the word of God and cannot, therefore, be false. But the Gospel narratives sometimes conflict and so far as they do they cannot be true in every detail, and if not true then not divinely revealed.[1] Moreover, there are apocryphal gospels excluded from the canon. The selection and validation of the canonical writings cannot be attributed afresh to divine revelation without question-begging or appeal to an infinite regress. It must depend on rational human judgement. If that is the criterion in one case, it must also be the criterion in the other. We must, therefore, seek to validate claims on historical grounds and this would be so even if the claim to divinity were based on miracle, for the occurrence of the miraculous could not be established except on historical evidence.

In this case, however, the historical evidence is exceedingly hard to come by. Such as we have is scanty, obscure and overlaid by legend and superstition. The documents themselves are not originals, the originals were not contemporary with the

---

[1] As revealing transcendent truths in symbolic form to peoples who could understand them in no other way, and as phases in the development of religious ideas which continuously progresses towards an ultimate truth, the scriptures are nevertheless accurately described as divinely inspired. But they are not distinguished, in that respect, from other writings of great genius and insight.

events they record but were written a generation or more after the death of Jesus, and by authors who are not known to have been eyewitnesses of the events or to have had personal acquaintance with the chief participant in them. The authors were not scholars nor scientists and were liable to all the superstitions current at the time. They had at their disposal no critical tradition or established method for determining the truth of rumours and verbal reports, and no established science to distinguish the factually possible from the fantastic. Their sincerity is manifest from their writing and is unquestioned, and undoubtedly they believed implicitly what they set down. But not even that has come to us intact or unaltered. It has been copied uncounted times and translated into diverse languages; errors have been incorporated and corrected from sources not themselves certain; additions have been made by unknown hands, and the originals have been recast with varying interpretations.

Nevertheless, there is evidence enough to put certain facts beyond reasonable doubt. That Jesus lived and taught in Judea in the reign of the Emperor Augustus, came into conflict with the priestly hierarchy of the Jews, was accused by them before the proconsul, Pontius Pilate, and was crucified. The general character and much of the detail of his teaching is also clear to us, as well as the nature of his personality and the profound effect it had upon his associates. Certain incidents recorded are so in keeping with these general facts and cohere so closely with his character and his main doctrines, that they stand out with the verisimilitude of a portrait by a great master. For example, the episode of the woman taken in adultery, and his rebuke to Peter for using violence to defend him against arrest. When allowance has been made for all the inconsistencies and doubtful points within the record, there still stands out from its pages a personality of overwhelming moral and spiritual power which shines through the mist of uncertainties like the morning sun.

III

Criticism of Jesus' moral teaching is the most serious challenge
to his divinity and must be met if his messianic mission is to be
substantiated. Christian morality has been attacked by many and
from many quarters, but whether and how far these attacks are
justfied is not relevant to the assessment of Jesus' personal teaching. The propriety or ineptitude of what St. Paul or the later
Church have added is not here in question. It may or may not
be a logical extension of the original. All that is pertinent to
our present inquiry is what Jesus himself said and what he
meant by it, and how his conduct bore out in practice what he
preached. We must try, therefore, to isolate his own precept
from his followers' and interpreters', and to sift out glosses on
and additions to his reported sayings by later copyists, as well
as by the authors themselves of the Gospels.

(1) A typical characteristic of Jesus' method was to seize
upon current beliefs and expectations, to adapt them to new
moral concepts and to give them new significance. The Jews of
the day were restive under the foreign yoke, they remembered
Judas Maccabeus and looked again for a national deliverer.
The coming of God's Kingdom was generally expected; but it
was understood as a national and political liberation, the reestab-
lishment of the traditional theocracy presided over by the House
of David. Jesus made the coming of the kingdom the central
theme of his preaching but gave it an entirely different sense.
He preached no secular rebellion or temporal revolution. His
kingdom was not of this world, not to be won with the sword.
It was within men's hearts—a kingdom of the spirit.

The phrase 'not of this world' has misled many into thinking
that he meant it was elsewhere, in a heaven above the skies.
But it takes little moral insight or intellectual penetration to see
that his real intention was to divert men's longings from temporal, impermanent and perishable objects to self-conquest,
purity of heart and selfless living. His exhortation, despite the
language in which it is often cast, is not to other-worldliness but
to present righteousness, the love and service of neighbours, and

to devotion to God through compassion and charity to men. The 'reward' for such conduct is spiritual not material. It is the good life itself, to which 'good living' in the sensual and material sense is at best instrumental and at worst detrimental—detrimental especially when pursued as an end in itself and not simply as a means.

Once it is recognized that the Kingdom of God is within you,[1] it must equally be apparent that the heaven, where neither moth nor rust corrupt, and where thieves do not break through nor steal, where the treasure of the righteous is laid up, is also 'within you', in the heart. It is the peace that the world of business and politics cannot give, the blessedness of the knowledge and love of what surpasses and sublates all temporal benefits— the love of God which is the essence of wisdom. Again, the pictorial language must not mislead us into thinking of a heaven elsewhere, beyond the stars, another temporal world of business and politics of a different sort. That is a complete misconception, is wholly inept and irrational, and the evidence we have is sufficient to assure us that it was not Jesus' true intention. It should not be surprising, however, that he used language and imagery that would appeal to the audience he addressed while it gave new meaning to the beliefs which they commonly entertained.

(2) Objection has been raised against Jesus' injunction to 'take no thought for your life, what ye shall eat and what ye shall drink; nor yet for your body, what ye shall put on', as giving too little weight to material goods and comfortable living,[2] and the complaint has been made that his opposition to wealth and 'glorification' of poverty is excessive.[3] At the same time it is generally admitted that he was no ascetic and his enemies reproached him as 'a man gluttonous and a wine-bibber' and as eating with publicans and sinners. What is surely obvious is that he did not overlook the material goods but recognizing

[1] An alternative rendering is 'among you', which must mean in your midst as a community, a Kingdom realized by your attitudes to and treatment of one another, and so just as much 'within you'.
[2] Cf. B. Blanshard. *Reason and Belief*, p. 336, and p. 338f.
[3] *Ibid.*

their instrumental value stressed the evil of treating them as ultimate and sufficient. Wealth also he did not condemn outright, for he had rich men among his friends and followers, Nicodemus and Joseph of Arimathea; but he was clearly aware of its inordinate allure and the temptation it offers as an end in itself. 'How hard is it for them that trust in riches to enter into the Kingdom of God'.

The answer to the rich young man who asked what he should do to inherit eternal life, that he should sell all he had and give it to the poor and follow Jesus, is not and could not be a universal injunction. The young man was obviously devout, eager to do right and well-given. 'Jesus, beholding him loved him'. He detected his weakness—'One thing thou lackest'—and admonished him accordingly. It was a personal exhortation not a general one. And the whole conversation is instructive because the first answer was simply to obey the commandments. This is the general requirement. But the morality of perfection which goes beyond the call of duty, disinterested benevolence and selfless devotion, is what brings complete salvation, that fulfilment which neither moth nor rust can corrupt nor thieves carry away. Jesus was not condemning wealth so much as commending generosity and self-giving.

To say that the Gospel glorifies poverty is an exaggeration and a mistake. The alleviation of poverty is commended and alms-giving, if in the right spirit and not simply for ostentation, approved. What Jesus emphasizes is that poverty is, of itself and apart from its effects, not evil. It is felt to be a hardship only if it is extreme (and extreme destitution is not praised anywhere in the Gospel) or if one's desires and aims are directed at material enjoyment, which are no part of virtue and even when gained tend to prove dissatisfying. To the covetous and avaricious poverty is oppressive, to those whose wants are simple, whose interests are not in bodily pleasures, but primarily in the welfare of others, their own possessions are of secondary importance. To be contented with a modest sufficiency is both a virtue and a source of happiness. Poverty is thus no obstacle to goodness, accords with humility (of which more presently) and is compatible with virtue which brings greater satisfaction than luxury. The commendation of poverty is more properly that of a rational and balanced sense of values. The good Samaritan is held up as a model not because he is poor (for he is not so depicted) but because of the generosity with which he attends to and pays for the care of the man fallen among thieves. The object is not to praise poverty so much as moderation and the proper use of wealth. Dives was not simply rich but also selfish and profligate. He did not, when alive, take heed of Moses and the Prophets. Lazarus was poor but guileless. Not his poverty but his good-heartedness stood him in stead.

In all this Jesus' teaching is closely in accord with that of the Greek philosophers, a fact overlooked by those who contrast the Christian with the Hellenic approach to ethics. In the *Apology* Socrates is represented as saying,

'For I do nothing but go about persuading you all, old and young alike, not to take thought for your persons or your properties, but first and chiefly to care about the greatest improvement of the soul. I tell you that virtue is not given by money, but that from virtue comes money and every other good of man, public and private.'

How near this comes to the Sermon on the Mount.

'Therefore take no thought saying What shall we eat? or, What shall we drink? or Wherewith shall we be clothed? (For after all these things do the Gentiles seek). For your heavenly Father knoweth that ye have need of these things. But seek ye first the kingdom of God and his righteousness; and all these things shall be added unto you.'

Socrates was notoriously neglectful of his own personal and family affairs, of his appearance and his raiment. He made light and even boasted of his poverty and he constantly rebuked luxury and intemperance. In the *Republic*, Plato commends what Glaucon calls 'a city of pigs' because it restricts its citizens to the healthy necessities of life and shows no interest in 'luxuries'. And when the luxuries are admitted they are confined to the labouring and producing class but strictly forbidden to the Guardians and their auxiliaries. Even then excessive wealth as well as poverty are to be excluded, and temperance is defined in similar terms to justice. Could Plato have fulfilled Professor Blanshard's[1] wish by writing a dialogue between Socrates and Jesus he would most likely have presented them in close agreement.

(3) Another point of convergence between Greek and Christian morality is the condemnation of pride (*hubris*), the vain imagination of man that he can equal and take the place of God. For the Christian (as we saw) this is the root of sin and evil. Pride is not just self-respect, which is a virtue and an essential factor in human dignity. It is the self-aggrandizement and self-conceit which rejects and refuses that sense of finitude and failure, which (as we also saw) recognizes and reverences the infinitely transcendent by which it knows its own limitations. The opposite of pride and its remedy is this very confession of finitude and failure. It is humility, the foundation of virtue and righteousness, as pride is of sin. 'What doth the Lord require of thee, but to do justly and to love mercy and to walk humbly with thy God', wrote Micah long before Luke put into the mouth of Mary the hymn which declared 'He hath put down the mighty from their seat and exalted the humble and meek'. Jesus extols the humble: 'Blessed are the poor in spirit for theirs is the kingdom of heaven'. But humility is thought by the critics to be the least admirable and most unreasonable of characteristics. Nietzsche and Oswald Spengler inveigh against it as despicable weakness, and even Blanshard's more measured judgement, which acknowledges the virtue of humility, finds an inconsistency in Jesus' teaching and claims with his own precept. He takes exception to Luke's parable of the master commanding his servant after a day's hard work to prepare food and wait upon him (the master) before refreshing himself. This conduct, says Blanshard, Jesus seems to approve, though it is the reverse of humility. But surely the point of the parable has been missed.

[1] *Op. cit.*, p. 34.

There is even a tone of disapproval in the narration, but its true moral is that we should be humble, whatever our service to God, and account ourselves unworthy. The implication is that 'ye' men behave in the high-handed manner of the master, whereas you should be like the servant willing, humble, devoted, giving more than is demanded.

On the other hand, Jesus himself never behaved like a tyrant or arrogant master of servants. 'I call you not servants, for the servant knoweth not what his lord doeth: but I have called you friends . . .'

Blanshard asserts further that Jesus' claim to be the son of God and the saviour of the world is the opposite of humility. But it is not a claim that he ever seems to have made for himself. Others made it for him, and although he is never (but once by implication) represented as repudiating it, he calls himself 'Son of Man', and when addressed as 'Good Master', rejects the title 'Why callest thou me good? None is good save one, that is God'. In any case, in his day, 'Son of God' meant no more than 'beloved of God', and was applied generally to any eminently good man. To call God the Father of humanity was nothing extraordinary, and in this sense sonship would naturally apply to Jesus as to others. He never clearly applied it directly to himself in any other sense.

The passages in which Jesus is reported as referring to 'the Son' are mostly ambiguous. In some cases they may be quite general, having the nature of parable and referring to relations in any household between father and son: 'The servant abideth not in the house forever: but the son abideth forever'. Moreover, it must not be forgotten that any genuine quotation of this kind is recorded by a writer initially convinced both that Jesus was the Son of God, in a supernatural sense of that phrase, and that he himself knew that he was. The Gospel of St. John where most of the passages occur in which Jesus is represented as referring to himself as God's son, opens with an unqualified statement of the doctrine that he was 'the only begotten of the Father', so it is natural that its author should give this sense to any reference to sonship which occurs in the narrative. Finally, these records were copied and rewritten time and again by men convinced of the doctrine, and they would have interpreted any statement seeming to refer to sonship as a positive claim to divinity.

(4) Another major criticism that has been made against Christian morality in general and Jesus' teaching in particular is of its pacifism. We may leave aside, in the present context, the concurrent criticism of the Christian Church for its militancy and persecution of reputed heretics. The reprehensibility of that, as inconsistency at least, is hardly to be denied; but here we are concerned only with the implications of the precepts not to resist evil and to turn the other cheek. That it is better and more reasonable to return good for evil and benefit for injury should not be disputed by any careful thinker. Socrates and Plato held the view[1] and the inveterate rationalist, Spinoza,[2] deduced it from the nature of human emotion and imagination. But does that imply refusing to resist force with force, or to restrain violence by violent means? In fact it does not. Jesus tells us not to respond to malicious acts with malice, to ill-temper with ill-temper, to injustice with injustice. He urges us to forgive, but not to condone. To restrain violence by force is not, however, necessarily to return evil for evil, and condign punishment for wrong-doing is not injustice. There is no conflict, therefore, between legitimate police action in a civilized state and Christian forgiveness and mercy (as is sometimes alleged), so long as punishment is not vindictive or savage.

The argument that international order would be impossible on Christian principles though often urged, is quite unfounded. That international methods and policies, past and present have been altogether unchristian is scarcely deniable, and while inter-state relations continue to be a matter of power politics they will remain so. But the maintenance of order in world affairs depends on principles similar to those operative in civic matters

---

[1] *Republic,* I, 335, and *Gorgias,* 508–9.
[2] Cf. *Ethics,* III, xlii, xliii.

and Christian morality, is so far from incompatibility with civic order, that it would, if observed, guarantee it unfailingly. First, we must stress that nothing in the sermon on the mount forbids us 'to punish the wrong doer and protect the children of the poor'. Secondly, if the rules were observed by all to return good for evil, to love one's neighbor and to serve one's fellow-man unstintingly, to seek neither advantage for oneself over others nor demand return for benefits offered, there would be no evil to restrain and no injustices to mitigate. That may well be too much to expect of sinful human nature; but if it is, the exhortations of Jesus do not prevent the firm maintenance of civil order by the forcible restraint and punishment of violators, so long as that is just, merciful and carried out in a spirit of concern as much for the welfare of the trespasser as for those trespassed against.

Two corollaries follow: one is that Jesus was by no means indifferent to civic virtue. That one should render unto Caesar the things that are Caesar's (that is, the legitimate demands of the state) in no way prevents one's rendering unto God the things which are God's. The performance of civic duty is a precondition of civilized order and the basis of morality. But the duties of my station in society do not exhaust the requirements of moral excellence. The former may be performed habitually, mechanically and from the wrong motives, so that more is required than their actual execution. There are, besides, those services and acts of benevolence which no civic law or function has a right to demand, but which will sweeten the life of others and enhance the harmony of everyone's existence.

The second corollary is that Jesus' rebuke of evil-doers, of hypocrites and oppressors is not inconsistent with his own teaching of love and tolerance. It is neither vindictive nor unjust. It is a warning and call to repentance, not vituperation or spite. Love of the sinner does not imply tolerance of the sin or condonation of his guilt. Forgiveness is always conditional on penitence, and to refrain from censure where it is merited is not to benefit the iniquitous. Love may well be expressed in reprimand and pardon can still follow on remorse.

Many have criticized Jesus' condemnation of the Scribes and the Pharisees and such acts as his cursing of the fig-tree, as incompatible with his teaching of compassion and love. Some have objected likewise to his threats of hell-fire and destruction of the wicked. But these are no obstacles to the claim we are defending. The fig-tree legend is probably distorted—possibly the misinterpretation of a parable, or some other saying, in conjunction with a coincidence exaggerated by a credulous chronicler. In connexion with a pronouncement on the power of faith, Jesus had apparently used the blight of the fig-tree as an example in some way. That he had cursed it for failing to give fruit out of season is most unlikely, for it would have been neither reasonable nor consistent. Would he who had fasted forty days without complaint have petulantly withered a fig-tree for failing to assuage a momentary pang of hunger, when it would have been as easy miraculously to produce figs before they were due? This is one more example of the irrelevance and the unenlightening character of miracle stories.

The castigation of the Scribes and the Pharisees is a condemnation of hypocrisy, self-righteousness and self-seeking, the punishment for which is its own frustration of the goodness intrinsic in friendship and love—the misery of secret heartburnings and the canker of mutual jealousies. Jesus never treated the Pharisees as enemies, though they often regarded him as theirs. He denounced their practices and warned them of the consequences to themselves, but he did not retaliate against their attacks nor resist their machinations. Finally he died for their sakes as for all others. His conduct and teaching throughout remain mutually consistent. The destruction of the wicked is what is inherent in their own action. To be wicked is *ipso facto* to be spiritually lost and to suffer the self-torment that attends upon persistent envy and rancour. No more may be meant and no more should be rightly understood, by 'hell fire', if it is not just a lurid mistranslation or a gratuitous addition by later copyists. On the other hand, to love God and man, to seek peace and the Kingdom of Heaven is itself the very way to salvation.

(5) Even so, some even sympathetic critics have been wor-

ried by the parables of the unjust steward,[1] of the talents[2] and of the man who paid his hired servants, not according to their efforts and deserts but as he had arbitrarily decided.[3] These stories display, so it is said, a primitive or even perverse sense of justice and, at best, encourage a corrupt morality for interested motives. Again we must be warned that the stories may not have come down to us in the form that they were originally told, nor can we be sure of the circumstances to which they were relevant. This seems to be the case with the first of these parables, for it seems internally inconsistent, and the moral, that he who is unfaithful in the least is also unfaithful in much, and who is unjust in little is unjust in much, discredits the advice to make friends with the mammon of unrighteousness. Probably the true form of the parable was different and its clear lesson was intended to be that one cannot faithfully serve two masters. If you serve mammon you must forsake God and look to mammon for your reward. But even if in so doing you earn high esteem among men, in the sight of God, who knows your heart, you will be an abomination. Here there is no distorted sense of justice and no encouragement of interested motives.

The parable of the talents is not an adjuration to greed and pandering to an employer's avarice, but, by analogy, a warning against wasting or leaving idle one's natural abilities. He who makes the most of his natural gifts gains proportionately more credit and satisfaction than he who neglects them and in consequence loses even his original capacities. The naturally skilled artist who exercises his talent becomes expert and possibly eminent, while one who is equally gifted but neglects to practise loses his ability. 'To every one that hath shall be given . . . but from him that hath not shall be taken away even that which he hath'.

The moral of the story of the hired servants and their payment is, perhaps, more recondite, but still apparent. So far as the kingdom of heaven is concerned, 'they also serve who only

[1] *Luke*, XVI, 1-15.
[2] *Matt.* XXV, 14-29.
[3] *Matt.* XX, 1-16.

stand and wait'. The opportunity to labour may come late in life but for that the servant is no less worthy. 'Why stand ye here all the day idle? . . . Because no man hath hired us'. They that have born the heat and burden of the day are also recompensed and are not unjustly treated, but the total scheme and how each contributes to it is known only to God, and man's claim to a reward depends solely on him. Again, we may interpret this to mean that the reward of virtue is not quantitative but is a spiritual satisfaction irrespective of time and opportunity.

It is surely obtuse to read the parable of the treasure hidden in a field[1] as the description of an act of trickery in the way Warner Fite, quoted by Blanshard, has done. The kingdom of heaven is like a pearl of great price, something for which all lesser goods may be joyfully sacrificed. A man who discovers a treasure in a field will pay any price he can muster for it. The essential point is that the discoverer sells all that he has to acquire the treasure, and the implication is that it is a treasure of a different kind and another sort of value from the possessions sold. It is less easy to explain why the discovery should be hidden ('which when a man hath found he hideth'), unless it is that one who merits such treasure does not crow about it, as the truly generous when they give alms let not their left hand know what their right hand doeth.

The story of the maniac who called himself Legion and the destruction of the Gadarene swine has been yet a further stumbling block for cavillers. Clearly the episode could not have occurred exactly as it is described. Today we know that insanity is not possession by devils nor cured by their expulsion, but in those days and long after it was the generally accepted opinion. Whatever the cause of the mental disturbance of the madman, Jesus' converse with him calmed him and restored him to sanity. At the same time, the herd of swine rooting nearby took fright, as likely as not from the excitement of the crowd of spectators at what they saw as a miracle. Possibly the panic of the animals

---

[1] *Matt.* XIII, 44.

was increased by well-meaning but excessive efforts to head them off from the cliff, over which, in the event, they stampeded. In all probability Jesus made some remark comparing the terror of the swine to the madness of the man he had cured, referring to it as an evil spirit, and perhaps the swineherds themselves, to exonerate themselves from neglect of their charge, invented the story of his permitting the evil spirits to enter the swine.[1] The report would naturally become embellished and exaggerated as it passed from mouth to mouth, and the disciples would readily have believed it, but the true facts could not give pretext for alleging that Jesus was indifferent to the safety of the animals or the interests of their owner; for whatever the true facts are they cannot be that he gave permission to demons to take possession of the beasts.

(6) It has further been charged against Jesus' teaching that he ignored or depreciated goods which a rational man should value. Of these the least in importance and the easiest to dispose of are the goods of physical prowess and well-being.[2] in belittling the 'things of this world' Jesus is held to have undervalued health, strength and athletic skills (among other things). It is clearly not so if rationality is preserved. A man who spent much of his time healing the sick is hardly one who undervalued health. Strength and athletic skills again, are natural gifts which we can cultivate (except as we can any natural talent), as little as we can, by taking thought, add a cubit to our stature. And we should do so, rationally, only so far as required for health and recreation. There can be little doubt that Jesus would not have approved the exaggerated cult of sport of our own day and the substitution it involves of means for ends. It is we who overvalue the goods involved in these accomplishments.

Did Jesus neglect or underrate the goodness of intellectual achievement and the intellectual virtues? 'Thou hast hid these things from the wise and prudent,' he is reported to have said,

[1] Cf. the version of the incident in *By an Unknown Disciple*, Anon. (London, 1919), Ch. I.
[2] Cf. Blanshard, *Reason and Belief*, p. 337.

'and revealed them unto babes'.[1] Again we must remember the circumstances and the intention of the statement. It is not to belittle the wise so much as to draw attention to the insight of the uninstructed (the disciples and the ordinary populace in contrast with the Scribes and the Pharisees—there is also just a touch of sarcasm in the reference to 'the wise and the prudent'). Furthermore, Jesus for the most part is addressing the unlearned. His concern is moral and not scientific, his message is prophetic not philosophical, and he knew as well as Aristotle that 'pure intellect moves nothing', or as Spinoza that 'nothing positive, which a false idea has, is removed by the presence of a true idea'.[2] Conduct depends as much on emotion as on knowledge; it is a matter of feeling and action, and only good emotions can counteract bad ones.

Spinoza maintained that prophecy aimed solely at the practical and at moral reformation, for which intellectual excellence was not indispensable. If it were, the vast majority of the human race would be excluded from the possibility of salvation. The appeal of prophecy is, therefore, primarily to the imagination.[3] Spinoza was firmly convinced of the power of the intellect, yet he admitted that prophecy could reveal religious truth through the medium of the imagination, and that the prophet neither is nor need be scientist nor philosopher. Jesus, he held was unique among prophets in that he revealed the nature of God, not only in his words but in his life and person. If this is so, we should not expect him to appeal to science or philosophy. He addressed the multitude and his own disciples, who were not scholars, and he conveyed the truths he wished to communicate through images and stories of the most familiar objects and events. He did so, moreover, with consummate skill which bespeaks an artistry and intelligence of surpassing excellence.

Socrates, to whom few would deny intellectual power or philosophical interest, is depicted by Plato as illustrating his arguments by the most simple and familiar analogies and examples.

[1] *Luke*, X, 21. Cf. also *Matthew*, XI, 25 and XXI, 16.
[2] Cf. also *Ethics*, IV, xiv.
[3] Cf. *Tractatus Theologico-Politicus*, Ch. I.

It is from the skills of carpenters, money-lenders and horse-trainers that he infers his conclusions about virtue and goodness. Here again there is similarity between Jesus and the man generally reputed to be the founder of western philosophy. Why then should we be unduly concerned lest Jesus should lack intellectual prowess or interest, or hold it against him that he failed to emphasize it? Once more, we must not overlook the fact that the Gospel-writers were not learned men and would probably have had no interest in or understanding of intellectual issues. Nevertheless, they have left us the picture of a man with unerring moral and psychological insight, a man of great genius and versatility in imaginative representation, of unassailable integrity and immeasurable inspiration.

Aesthetic achievement (which Jesus has sometimes been said to lack or neglect) cannot be separated from religion, for in great measure religion and art are indistinguishable. Not only does great art present religious subject matter (witness the tragedies of Sophocles and innumerable paintings of the great masters), but religion *pur sang* expresses itself in parable and poetry and its monuments are works of art. The parables of Jesus and much of the Gospel writing are literature of the highest order, and only the insensitive or unperceptive could complain of failure in this respect.

IV

Once we have laid these doubts to rest we can appreciate the true genius and supreme inspiration of Jesus' moral doctrine. To see it in its fulness and essential quality one must turn to the sermon on the mount. Here we find values ranged in their true order, spirit exalted above legal formalism, motive and sincerity above ostentation, service and devotion above mercenariness.

The sermon on the mount sums up all moral teaching and all law.[1] Its persistent guiding-thread is the call for service, sacrifice and love of one's neighbour, without which, in the final

[1] Cf. my *Revelation through Reason*, Ch. V.

issue, society, which is the matrix of human achievement, cannot accomplish its ends. The performance by each member of the duties of his or her station is certainly indispensable, and if conscientiously carried out may achieve much. But by itself this is not enough. There is a prior and more essential condition of the unfailing discharge of those duties. The ends of society are attainable only through the mutual co-operation of its members acting in community, and if that is given grudgingly, social welfare will proportionately be frustrated. If men co-operate only from self-interest they do so imperfectly and only within limits. If they are forced to do what society requires, they do it from fear of penalties, and so will attempt whenever they can to evade both their duty and the consequences of neglecting it. The results are corruption and social failure. But co-operation from love of one's neighbour is unstinting and free. If it were universal it would be the remedy for all social ills. It strengthens ties, it eliminates suspicion, it generates (while it also tempers) zeal, and it is the foundation of concord. Paul in the 15th. chapter of the first epistle to the Corinthians accurately describes its qualities, for only in charity is faith objectified and hope substantiated.

The teachings of all the great moralists before and after Jesus do little more, in principle, than converge on his. Socrates, we have already noted, taught a similar doctrine. Even the dictum that virtue is knowledge converges, in its development by Socrates and Plato, with the doctrine of love. For the knowledge which is virtue is, in the last resort, knowledge of the Good, as it is equally the love of Beauty, a Form difficult, in Plato's writing, to distinguish from the Good; and the Good is what makes all things intelligible, all minds intelligent, the origin and sustainer of all existence. How does this differ from the love of God conceived as we have sought to conceive him in these pages? And it is in the light of that conception that the love of God redeems, that God and Christ are one and that he who taught the gospel of love revealed the means of grace.

Both Plato and Aristotle found their ethical doctrine on the recognition of the person as of primary value. In the *Republic* it is a person's native ability that determines his place in society and his consequent rights. For Aristotle likewise it is virtue and civic excellence, not birth or wealth that determines political desert. But this respect for persons, the devotion and love of human beings for their own sakes, is carried to its final conclusion only in the sermon on the mount.

Spinoza summed up the essential and universal religion in similar terms, as the belief that God exists, is one, is immanent in all things and has dominion over everything, and that the worship of God consists solely in obedience to his law, solely in justice, charity and the love of one's neighbour.

Kant's principle, that you should treat humanity, in your own person as well as in the persons of others, as an end in itself and never merely as a means, is but a restatement of Jesus' second law: 'Love thy neighbour as thyself.'

This again is the rational basis of the liberal doctrine of the equality of man, stemming from John Locke and Rousseau, and followed by the framers of the United States Constitution. Liberty, equality and fraternity and all the principles of democratic polity are derivative from, as they are surpassed by, the gospel of love, service and self-giving, without which mutual trust is undermined and political corruption erodes the ideals which statesmen and philosophers have set before the nations.

Not even love of one's neighbour is the limit of Jesus' admonition. He exhorts further to love of one's enemies. This imperative may be called a benign paradox, for if it were universally respected, the treatment of enemies as if they were friends would remove their enmity. Hostility engenders vicious emotions and generates false ideas (stereotypes) of opponents. Love of one's enemies would dispel all these and replace them with benevolent feelings and charitable opinions. In these precepts is the healing of all discord and the consolidation of communal activity. This is the bed-rock that sustains the Kingdom of God, devotion to which before all else is the essence of Jesus' teaching. It is the morality of perfection, going beyond the mere performance of what is due, exceeding the demands of common decency and

superseding justice itself—for, as Aristotle declared, friends have
no need of justice.

The principles of this morality were objectified and illustrated
in Jesus' own life and practice. He forgave his detractors without condoning their faults. He did not resist evil nor oppose
force by force. Where he condemned he also pitied. He treated
all persons with equal respect, irrespective of their station and
even when he had occasion to rebuke their misdeeds. He showed
no resentment against persecution or vilification, but met all
hostility with patience and forbearing. His adjuration to be
perfect as your Father in heaven is perfect he himself fulfilled.

So Jesus taught and so lived, and to do likewise is to unite
man with God. To reveal this to mankind is to be a redeemer,
for God and Christ are one. As Christ, Jesus is one with God,
but as man he is a finite manifestation of the spirit of God.
Thus he takes manhood into God without reducing the Godhead to the level of flesh. It is therefore futile to contend that
his lack of omniscience is inconsistent with divinity. In any case,
many of the errors and misunderstandings (in the light of modern knowledge) attributed to Jesus by Blanshard (op. cit.,
p. 384, for instance) are specious: e.g., to cite David as author
of a psalm, now thought to have been written by a different
hand, is hardly an error when the reference is being quoted
against the Scribes, who knew no better. Jesus' concern was not
literary criticism but spiritual enlightenment. It is alleged by
Bertrand Russell (in *Why I am not a Christian*), and also by
Blanshard, that much of his teaching, especially his prescription
to take no thought for the morrow, was conditioned by the false
belief that the end of the world was at hand, which he is said
to have shared with his disciples and others of his day. But there
is scant evidence that he held any such belief, even though some
of his followers undoubtedly did; and the injunction has been
otherwise explained above. The promises to the disciples that
they should 'not have gone over the cities of Israel till the Son
of Man be come' is ambiguous and has no clear reference to a
second coming. It could mean to predict no more than the reve-

lation to the people thus proselytized of the divinity of Christ.[1]

Consequently, to point to the limitation of Jesus' outlook and knowledge, bounded as it must have been by the nature and experience of the society in which he lived, and to present this as evidence against his divinity, on the ground that deity implies omniscience—such argument is simple misunderstanding of the doctrine of atonement. The Christ, we have shown, must be both man and God. Had the knowledge and accomplishments of Jesus not been limited to human dimensions, to those of a man living in his historical period, he would *not* have been both man and God—'One; not by conversion of the Godhead into flesh, but by taking of the manhood into God.'

The Holy Spirit, which proceeds from Christ as from God, speaks and is manifest in the person of Jesus. So it is that Jesus is the head of that mystical body of Christ (the pleroma of which St. Paul writes and which Teilhard expounds), of which all are members who follow his behest and possess his spirit. So it is that he is first in the spiritual kingdom, the union of hearts and minds that we have found to be essential to the conception of deity in a theistic outlook. This union, at least in one aspect, constitutes the supra-personality of a triune God: creator, saviour and the holy spirit which is active in both creation and redemption, in both redeemer and redeemed.

In this way we have essayed to explicate more fully the conception of a spiritual whole, transcendent and self-complete, which is implicit in the forms of nature and humanity, and which forces humanism and pantheism beyond their immediate limits to theism proper—a theism which when fully explicated leads to the essential elements of Christian belief.

---

[1] Christ understood as redeemer—the present consciousness and love of God, taught and manifested by Jesus.